WINNING VICTORY

IN

SPIRITUAL WARFARE

BY ANNE S. WHITE

Winning Victory in Spiritual Warfare, by Anne S. White
ISBN # 089-228-128-6

Copyright © 1998 by Anne S. White

Victorious Ministry Through Christ, Inc.
P.O. Box 1804, Winter Park, Florida 32790

Distributed by **Impact Christian Books, Inc.**
332 Leffingwell, Suite 101,
Kirkwood, MO 63122

And

Victorious Ministry Through Christ
P.O. Box 1804
Winter Park, FL 32790

Printed in the United States of America

DEDICATION

This book is gratefully dedicated to my wonderful family – and to all who have furthered the work of Victorious Ministry Through Christ (clergy and lay persons) whose very real commitments have enabled Jesus to use their time and gifts "to set the captives free, give sight to the blind and open prison doors"!

ALSO BY THIS AUTHOR:

HEALING ADVENTURE

DAYSPRING

THE TRANSFORMING POWER OF GOD

TRIAL BY FIRE

STUDY ADVENTURE IN TRIAL BY FIRE

JESUS, ALL IN ALL

FREED TO LIVE

HEALING DEVOTIONS

THE MASTER SPEAKS TODAY

TABLE OF CONTENTS

ACKNOWLEDGMENTS

My grateful thanks go to the many members of the Board of Directors of Victorious Ministry Through Christ. Over the past twenty-seven years, they have given spiritual covering, wise guidance and effective personal support to this God-given ministry as it grew in the Lord's purpose and timing. I give thanks for all the Board and Team Members (not only in the USA but also in eight other countries) whom the Lord has used to develop and spread VMTC to bless those in need of this special kind of healing. I thank God for the prayers of my Bishop and the five clergy of our Church as He has used their ministries to encourage and bless me as well as to cover my lay ministry. It would be impossible to name all of those who in so many different ways, at different times and in different countries have contributed to the victories that Jesus has won in unfolding and wisely establishing this ecumenical, international work of the Holy Spirit! Their names are written in heaven.

I give thanks for the wise, loving support of my late husband, Dick, who released me to the Lord and covered this ministry until the time he went Home to the Lord on February 15, 1974. His wise provision for me has enabled me ever since his death to serve God full-time over many years without remuneration – and without taking any income from my many speaking engagements and the sale of my nine books. I give thanks for our daughter and our son and his fine family – for their loving support in understanding and prayer over so many years.

I give thanks for the long-time commitment of Rev. Alva H. Brock (who faithfully served with me – first as VMTC's Vice-President, and more recently as President) and his wife, Bunny – to whom the Lord gave (on the morning of my husband's death) the prophecy concerning the future world-wide outreach of VMTC. I give thanks for my long-time "prayer partner" Loretta Moore, who traveled with me many times to three Far Eastern countries and has been a very important Lead Woman prayer minister – training thousands of clergy and lay people. Also, special thanks go to Nancy Zanazanian (whose reward has come only from the Lord) for serving cheerfully and effectively many years as Bookkeeper and Treasurer as well as "prayer partner" on the Board of Directors. Gratitude is expressed to Don and Edith Mercer who have been led to undergird VMTC faithfully over many years – not only with prayers and time-consuming ministry, but also with most generous financial help, as needed. Over the years, Dr. Denny Van Loan and Mrs. Laura Wygant have given outstanding support; and they paid their own airfares as they labored under most difficult conditions in our first trip to New Zealand. My appreciation goes to many others too numerous to name specifically! May God bless all of those who have shared with me in this adventure!

I am grateful for the helpful perspective and constructive criticism of those who carefully read this manuscript: Donna Watkins, Shy Mackes, Barbara Yocum, Evelyn Thames, Bill and Doris Buchhorn, and Dick and Sandy Dirks. Their prayers and encouragement have been most valuable as they urged me to press on to publication of this book. Donna Watkins has been especially patient and faithful in the typing and editing of this manuscript.

Throughout these many years, my daughter and son (and his wife) have always been lovingly supportive of my ministry and have never in any way been jealous of this "third child" or of my commitment to VMTC. Ever since Dick went Home to the Lord, they have made sure that I spent Christmas holidays with one or the other of them and usually with both! It has been a joy for me in late December to fly to Scotland (by way of Chicago where I have had a brief airport visit with Richard and Carolyn to exchange Christmas gifts). After flying on to Scotland, I have spent a Scottish Christmas with my daughter helping her entertain and being entertained by her many lovely friends – so that I feel a part of her very busy life. She is an Associate Principal in a well-known college near her lovely home. Early in January, I flew back to Chicago, bringing her gifts to Richard and his family. Carolyn has graciously had a second Christmas dinner for me and we have opened all the gifts with their now grown-up daughter and son. Sarah Anne is a senior and Danny is a freshman in college. I thank God for the wonderful family He has given me and for their constant, faithful support of me – especially during times when VMTC has had crises and I needed their loving prayers and wise "listening ears". Maryanna is an elder in the Church of Scotland and I enjoy worshiping with her at their services. Richard is an elder in the Presbyterian Church (USA) and both of my grandchildren have preached in their church at Youth Sunday services when they were in high school. I usually have spent the weekend with my son and his family on my way home from California, Michigan or Illinois Schools. Maryanna and I have enjoyed vacationing together in Alaska and Spain or touring Scotland by car. One year I was able to take Maryanna, Richard and Carolyn to Puerto Rico where we had a wonderful time. We all agreed that the only problem was that our time together was too short! How gracious the Lord has been to give me not only these two fine families but also my extended world-wide VMTC family!

Anne S. White

AUTHOR'S FOREWORD

For years, people have asked me to write an autobiography – but I have never felt the Lord's call to do that. In fact, I had decided not to write another book as I have nine in print. But a few months ago, the Lord began to anoint me to write – and as the words given me began to point to a history of Victorious Ministry Through Christ, I realized that His Will was for me to share the stories and insights that have come from "winning the victory in spiritual warfare". Two Board members confirmed this guidance. As this ministry was birthed and spread not only across the USA but also to many other countries, the warfare became more and more intensive. But, in each episode, the Lord increased my faith as I grew in total commitment to His Will. The Lord has been glorified as the enemy has been defeated over and over again in so many different ways and in different countries – as His Plan for VMTC unfolded. God's call was answered by thousands of clergy and lay people whose lives were changed as they experienced His healing release from bondages to persons, places, things and experiences – and (after being healed) became part of His healing ministry to others. The promise in Luke 4:18 and 19 really means that those who have been healed will be used to bring the Lord's healing to others.

Although Satan was defeated at Calvary, he is still trying to thwart God's Plan – so, we who are committed to Jesus, need to wage "spiritual warfare" and win the victory in His Name and to His Glory! May the Lord use this book to help each reader find the reality of God's Love in a new way. May your faith grow in Jesus' Power to win victories in your lives as He overcomes with His good what our adversary, Satan, intends for evil! May each of us respond to Jesus' commitment to us by accepting His challenge to become overcomers – not "spectator Christians" or "drop-out Christians" – but those whose lives can be used by Him to continue His healing ministry today. May the reality of transformed lives speak very loudly in today's world where the need is so great for us Christians to live the Word of God and "walk our talk," proclaiming in answered prayers the Good News that Jesus "sets the captives free, gives sight to the blind and opens prison doors" – when we are obedient to His call! May these spiritual principles become essential parts of our life styles – not just words of Scripture, but life-changing ministry – enabling us to make Jesus more fully Lord in the lives of those for whom He calls us to pray in today's spiritual warfare!

INTRODUCTION

For several years, those of us who have known and worked closely in VMTC ministry with Anne S. White have wanted her to write an autobiography of her exciting life in Christ. Now at last, led by the Holy Spirit, she has written this inspiring, encouraging book – telling of her own rich experiences in an anointed, interdenominational ministry of the Church called "Victorious Ministry Through Christ", which God founded through Anne and her late husband in 1971.

I have been a "partner in Christ" in VMTC Ministry with Anne since the early 1970's. I have found her to be a woman of steadfast faith, tremendous discipline, single-minded commitment to Christ and keen spiritual insights. The ministry she describes so well in this book is a Scriptural, proven, effective, balanced, accountable and life-changing ministry. It has been an instrument that has brought healing of relationships, assurance of forgiveness and new freedom in the Holy Spirit to many thousands of people over the last twenty-seven years – leading them into a much deeper commitment to Jesus Christ. I am one of those whose life has been wonderfully changed by this ministry. And I have ministered in this country and over seas to thousands of people whose lives have been changed by it – so that they could become more Christ-like. One of the strengths of VMTC is that it is a multiplication ministry since those who are blessed, so often want to be trained to do the ministry – it goes on and on and on, affecting many churches. This has been true not only in my own ministry, but also of many others in 8 countries where VMTC has been established.

What is so meaningful about this book is that in it, Anne opens some windows into her own life. She reveals the faith that her parents had while she was a child and how they taught her to pray and have faith. She reveals how in college she almost lost her faith and how in her hour of desperation with her son's illness and her deep need to be set free from unforgiveness, self-pity, and fear, God gave her the power to let go of these – so that healing and deliverance came. She reveals the experience of being baptized in the Holy Spirit and the supernatural Power that God gave her in Japan to fulfill the ministry He had for her there. She reveals how God, in the midst of much spiritual warfare, gave her the wisdom, with her husband's help, to establish "Victorious Ministry Through Christ"; and the power God gave her at the time of her husband's three heart attacks and later at his death. She reveals how God protected and guided her, giving victory in spiritual warfare as she took this ministry to eight countries around the world – and how God gave her the courage and strength to found it in local churches and maintain high standards at great cost. As she tells her remarkable faith-story, we find our own faith increasing. The theme of this book might well be expressed in the words of a chorus that we who have been a part of this Ministry have sung in our Training Schools and in our Mission trips overseas. "He is able, He is able. I know my Lord is able to carry me through. He heals the broken hearted. He sets the captives free. He opens wide the prison doors and causes the blind to see." This is a chorus based on *Isaiah 61:1-4* and *Luke 4:18-19*, the key Scriptures of VMTC Ministry. As you read this book, I believe you will see that Jesus is able to meet your needs as He met Anne's need, when you are willing to let Him. You, too, will "Win Victory In Spiritual Warfare"!

Rev. Alva H. Brock, President Emeritus
Victorious Ministry Through Christ

WINNING VICTORY IN SPIRITUAL WARFARE

CHAPTER I

HOW IT ALL BEGAN

Ensenada, as its name implies, was "a low land between mountains" – a very small town on the southeast coast of Puerto Rico. My parents had gone there in 1900 as my father was a civil engineer to take charge of all the building of an American owned sugar centrale. They had three small boys and were saving their money so they could send them to college some day in the States. The South Puerto Rico Sugar Company operated a two-room schoolhouse for their employees' children because the standards of native schools would not meet American college standards. My mother was a remarkable Southern woman who (although she had not been able to attend college) became our best teacher. She was a genius and was able to bring out in her children all the qualities with which God had endued them. When the two college graduates (employed by the company) came to teach each year, my mother would learn whatever subject was the teachers' weakest – and coach her children accordingly – so that my three brothers entered Cornell University (one at the age of fourteen) and graduated without ever going to mainland preparatory schools.

When finally, after waiting twelve years, my parents decided to try again for a girl, their prayers were answered. My oldest brother was sixteen and was studying hard to take

College Board exams. He and my two other brothers expressed their love for me by riding me over rock-piles in the baskets of their bicycles and teaching me how to read and write when they sat at a huge table studying their lessons! I remember them more like young uncles – and enjoyed being spoiled by them – within the limits of my disciplined parents' approval. I think I remember my grief when my oldest brother left home – and I well remember the few times we visited them after they went away to the States to Cornell University. When I was five years old, my mother took me to school – and the teacher entered me in the 3rd grade class because I already knew 1st and 2nd grade work!

My mother and father were the spiritual strength of the community. She superintended the Sunday School and they made sure that our little Mission Church had services every other Sunday night – one time, an Episcopal priest; and the other time, a Presbyterian Pastor from the nearest city which was one and a half hours away. Although I was brought up in a Christian home, I was never asked to give my life to the Lord or to join a Church. At fifteen, I graduated (the only one in my class) from High School and boarded a ship for the States – headed for two months at an excellent summer camp and four years at Wellesley College! My mother had taught me to pray, and when I had malaria aboard the ship with an exceedingly high temperature, I prayed and the Lord healed me – but I did not at that time make a commitment to Jesus. When I got to college and was exposed to Unitarian teachings of the community and "form criticism" of Bible teachers who did not believe in Jesus, my "second-hand faith" was quenched easily! About that time, my mother became involved in Christian Science – but to me, that was "gobbledegook"! She was searching for healing, and could not find a healing ministry in her Church –

so she wandered into several occult realms. (Praise God! Many years later I was able to lead her back to her faith in Jesus – and she died a believing Christian!) I really lost my faith because the miracles in the New Testament were being de-bunked by my professor, and the Old Testament was taught only as history – even though the Bible was required curriculum and Wellesley had been founded years ago as a Christian College. One thing, however, that influenced my life spiritually was our motto: "Not to be ministered unto but to minister."

After graduation, I was privileged to be the first woman ever employed by IBM – and (even in the depression) started my career with an excellent position in the Cincinnati office where I was to set up the accounting system and train all personnel who would be using IBM tabulating equipment. I would work with the Vice-President or Treasurer of a company that was a new customer to find out what reports were needed and then set up the system – working at that place until all problems were finally solved and the new accounting procedures were in effective use. Sometimes that meant working till 3:00 AM – if the machines had "glitched" and the necessary reports had not been produced! As the very expensive equipment was rented (not sold) the customer could throw out the whole system if results were not satisfactory and personnel were not well trained. At the age of nineteen, this was a very heavy responsibility! As soon as the new equipment and procedures were functioning effectively, I was transferred to a new client – to begin a similar process of installing the IBM system. One time it was at a furniture store, another at a meat packing company and still another time at a bank – and so on. It was a very strenuous pace with lots of responsibilities and never a dull moment! Little did I know that some day the Lord would use all of this training for *His* purposes – but that was to be revealed to me at a later date.

I had met my husband when I dated his room-mate (a distant cousin of mine) at the Naval Academy – and the following year, I went to June Week with Dick. It was a very exciting and glamorous occasion! We corresponded after he went out to the West Coast to join his ship. Dick had graduated from the Naval Academy and was commissioned an ensign but was unhappy during the subsequent one and a half years when he served on a cruiser on the West Coast (while I was still at Wellesley). For various reasons, he had decided to resign his commission and had taken a civilian position in Washington D.C. – much to my relief as I had not wanted to be a Navy wife and bring up "Navy brats". Dick and I were married at the end of the Summer and I moved from Cincinnati to take a position in charge of the statistical tabulating unit at FDIC. We had agreed that we would not have children for five years – and we were saving my salary to provide for their future college education.

After World War II broke out in Europe, Dick began to get letters from the U.S. Navy Department begging him to return to active duty. He had continued to serve as a Naval Reserve officer and felt very heavily the call of duty to our country – so finally he was re-commissioned and went on duty at the Navy Department in Washington D.C. Our daughter was only 8 months old when Pearl Harbor shattered the US Navy with devastating results! Three months later, Dick had to leave for anti-submarine duty in the South Atlantic – a real dislocation for us all! When I realized that another child was on the way, I felt very depressed about the hazards of war, the long separation and the inability to communicate with my husband

18

because of necessary Navy secrecy. "Loose lips, sink ships" was a warning heeded by all – so wives never knew where their husbands were in danger. My fears increased that Dick might not return alive! Our son was born on December 13, 1942 and a good friend of ours took me to the hospital while his wife took care of our daughter. As our two children were only 20 months apart in age, I was on constant duty! Two years later, Dick's father died of pneumonia complicated by a heart attack! This sudden shock left his mother in a very depressed state. As Dick was an only child, I felt the need to leave my parents in Miami (where I had moved to be near them because of my father's failing health) and move to Washington, D.C. to help my mother-in-law in her time of bereavement. My intentions were the best – but moving into winter weather and the crowded situation of two young children living in her antique-filled apartment put a great strain on us both. She was morbid over the sudden death of her husband and I was morbid over being totally out of touch with my husband under such trying circumstances – along with the fear which both of us had that Dick would be killed in action!

I'm sure that the emotional strain and bitterness that developed between us two neurotic women led to my contracting pneumonia and being hospitalized. I was terrified that I would also die (as civilians could not get needed medication) and our children would be left to her care! Cruel words made matters worse – and, after recovering at a very generous friend's lovely home when I was released from the hospital, the doctor advised me to move back to Florida. Miraculously, I was able to return to the same apartment building near where my parents lived – but my anger against my mother-in-law's ingratitude was still smoldering within me.

During those three years, I actually had three kinds of pneumonia – and my mother told me that I would die if I did not forgive my mother-in-law! What a relief it was when World War II ended and Dick returned home safely!

CHAPTER II

TWO MIRACLES OF GOD'S GRACE

After World War II ended, we had moved to Norfolk, VA and had survived all the dislocations of bringing a family back together again. But our son was severely handicapped by frequent asthmatic attacks which were causing him to be a hypochondriac as he could not play with other children on the many bad days that winter. It was 2:00AM as my 5 year old son was gasping for breath and I was alone with my fears! My husband was on his Navy ship thousands of miles away from home and there was no medication that I could give for this traumatic attack of asthma. That day our pediatrician had told me there was no medical cure – and that if our son ever outgrew the asthma, it would be seven more years. I was a desperate mother engulfed in hopelessness! The Lord in His mercy spoke to me with His still, small Voice and told me to kneel down and pray. To my amazement, He told me that it was *not* His will for an innocent child to suffer – that it was the result of my long-standing resentment against my mother-in-law and that I must forgive her. What I had not wanted to do for three years became a reality through His mercy and grace as I found myself saying, "I forgive her Lord" – and really meaning it! Then the still, small Voice continued: "If you really have

21

faith, you will thank Me before you see the answer". By His Grace I said, "Thank you, Lord" – and our son took one deep, peaceful breath – and has never had asthma since! Years later, Dick had orders to Navy duty in Japan, the worst climate for asthmatics. Praying as Abraham did about Issac, we made our decision to go – instead of requesting a change of orders. The Lord honored our faith and Richard had the healthiest year of his life in a climate where many grown servicemen had to be sent home because they were suffering such damaging, asthmatic attacks. To Him be the Glory!

The Lord had impressed two things on me at the time of this dramatic healing: a) He was not punishing our child for my sin, but rather my own resentment, fear and self-pity were creating a suffocating, spiritual climate. Though we had changed physical climates, the tensions I had caused in my home had moved with us! I was a "resentment-holic", a "fear-holic" and a "self-pity-holic". b) I would need to write a letter of apology to my mother-in-law (regardless of what she had said or done to me in the past) and invite her to visit us. I did – and she did! God honored this change of heart and taught me that my own spiritual healing in this broken relationship was as important as the physical healing of our son! In that encounter with Him, I had been blessed with *two miracles of His Grace*!

After this double healing experience, I committed my life to the Lord. I promised "to do whatever He asked me to do to help restore the healing ministry to His Church." We moved often – so my "spiritual pilgrimage" was constantly being interrupted – but God used each of those many moves to further my healing ministry. Dick had received orders to sea duty, so we moved to a very old, large, drafty house in Newport, RI – but then the Navy sent the destroyer he commanded to Key West, FL for winter training exercises! It always snowed heavily on Saturday night – so I struggled to shovel out our long driveway every Sunday morning so we could go to Church and Sunday School. A year later, as I had finally outfitted our children and myself with suitable wool suits and heavy coats for the long, bitter New England winters, the Navy decided to send Dick to the Armed Forces Staff College in Norfolk, VA for a three months' command course. So at Thanksgiving, we moved to Norfolk again! Because it was such a short tour of duty, our quarters were small and cramped. By Washington's Birthday, we were on the move again – this time to Houston, Texas – where all the children wore blue jeans! My frustration with the Navy increased over the expense of having to outfit our family again with new wardrobes. But, at least we were able to buy our first home! We were welcomed by friendly Texans and soon became joyously involved in our neighborhood Episcopal Church. While setting up, with my husband, a double Sunday School in that large Church and praying with the sick at Healing Services, the Lord led me into a deeper walk with Him!

However, a year or so later, Dick had completed his tour of duty in Houston where he had been in charge of expediting the Navy's tremendous oil shipments through the Ship Channel as they were badly needed to supply our forces in the war in Korea. We had sudden orders to move again to Norfolk! Our faith had been increasing and we were blessed as God worked a real miracle in selling our house very quickly. I wept my way out of our very loving Church where our Rector's contagious faith was helping to change our lives. He often said: "When you pray, move your feet!" His favorite words were: "Have faith!"

My frustration with the Navy increased as our family adjusted to new schools and new responsibilities and a Church that sadly was lukewarm. I began to have severe tension headaches and loss of equilibrium. At a Healing Service, the Lord healed me instantly of the vertigo when I asked Him to forgive me for my frustration with the Navy and my resentment over the many moves we had been forced to make. But, I found that I needed to maintain a new emotional life style. If I slipped back into the old frustrations, fears and resentments, I would have a recurrence of the symptoms. The Lord was teaching me a new life-style in which praise and thanksgiving were to replace my sins of self-pity and resentment. It was a conditional healing – depending on my abiding in Christ instead of abiding in the old pattern of destructive emotions. I learned to pray away my frustrations instead of wallowing in them. Praise changes things because it changes us – our perceptions and habit patterns. No wonder that there are so many Scriptures pointing us to the importance of praise and thanksgiving! We are to let our requests be known to God in praise – not in worry and doubt and bitterness. I found that I needed to start each day with a "quiet time" in which I could praise God for who He is and thank Him for His many blessings!

WINNING VICTORY IN SPIRITUAL WARFARE

CHAPTER III

EMPOWERED BY THE SPIRIT

In the Spring of 1952 as I was doing my usual homemaking chores one afternoon in Norfolk, VA, the Lord summoned me to stop and listen to Him. The still, small Voice of God informed me clearly that He was calling me to be a missionary. Before I could even ask where He was going to send me, I heard the word, "Japan"! My immediate protest was: "Lord, I hate the Japanese – look what they did to our ships in Honolulu when they sank so many, and killed so many innocent people without warning!" The quiet reply was firm: "I will give you My Love for the Japanese people." "But what about my children?", I replied. Again the still, inner Voice countered my evasion with: "When you are with them, *love* them". I was ashamed that I had not always been as loving as I should have been – but I was still thinking of excuses when I heard these words: "There will be a wonderful Japanese maid standing at the door when you arrive – waiting to carry in the bags. You are going to teach My Word where it has not been taught before. And you will help start a 'Theological School' in Japan." In utter dismay, I broke off this unexpectedly specific conversation and began to ponder all these words in my heart! I knew that I wanted to be the Lord's missionary – but this was all too preposterous as I was married and had two children, an 11 year old daughter and a son 20 months younger! How could I ever leave my family and traipse off to Japan? Two weeks went by and I had told no one of this spiritual encounter. Then my husband came home from his office with the news: "We have orders to Japan! I know you won't like it, so I'll call Washington and try to get the orders changed!" Those words reverberated through my mind and hurriedly I said: "O, please don't! I know it will be a good experience for the children!" At that point, I did not dare to share my encounter with God as my husband would have been sure that I was crazy!

Months went by – and before my husband sailed off to Japan, he moved the children and me back to Houston, as Navy housing in Tokyo would not be available for over a year. We decided that the children and I would be happiest if we returned to Houston to live near our former Church where we had so many friends. So, when school was out, we moved back from Norfolk – only to find that our former Rector was starting a *new* Mission Church in a *different* suburb! I felt that this would be good training for me so I offered my time and talents to become his unsalaried assistant in setting up the Sunday School and Women's Ministry – in fact, everything he did not have time to do! The Church grew from Mission status to a self-supporting Parish in about six months! In fact, the Bishop enthusiastically said it became a Parish before he could say, "Hallelujah"! At that time, he commented that I had "the enthusiasm of St. Peter and the faith of St. Paul"! The months dragged on interminably – but the Lord's Presence was sustaining me as we waited for housing in Japan to become available. Late in the Spring of 1953, I attended a Retreat in preparation for our impending move to Tokyo and the "missionary call" that the Lord had put on my life. In the prayer room, the Lord reminded me through my tears that I had accepted Him as Healer and Savior but not as my Lord and Master. This was two months before – and in preparation for a third milestone in my "spiritual adventure"!

When in July we finally received orders to sail to Japan, we packed our limited allowance of belongings – and the Church sent me off with books and clothing for the Japanese people. I prayed for the Lord to show me what I could take as I walked around our apartment – because (as we were to have furnished quarters) our weight allowance for shipping our possessions could not exceed 2,000 lbs! When the movers weighed our overseas shipment, the scale tipped at 1950 lbs! We had to leave everything else in storage in Texas.

The children and I began the long drive to San Francisco, crossing a desert on the way. One afternoon we had a sudden blowout and I was terrified as our Buick unexpectedly swerved out of control! I prayed for the Lord to give me strength to control it, to get to a safe stopping place on that rough shoulder. I looked up and there was a State Trooper smiling at me and saying, "Lady, can I help you?" He had noticed my tire and turned around to come back to change it and start me on my way again to San Francisco. How wonderful is God's Providence! After difficult driving in that hilly city, we finally got to the dock and boarded our transport safely (along with the car) much to my relief. A wave of thanksgiving came over me: God had brought us safely thus far in spite of my fears – and the ship would soon sail to take us 8000 miles across the Pacific Ocean to a strange country where we would join my husband at last! I was filled with excitement – but also fear of my inadequacy.

As the children dashed out of our cabin, eager to explore the ship which would be their home for 14 days, I knelt down to pray. Alone in my cabin, the Lord convicted me of my need to repent for my sins of thoughts, words and deeds as well as my sins of omission (the things that I had not done). At that moment I realized that I was powerless to fulfill God's Purposes for me to be a missionary, so I cried out to Him: "I might as well be a failure in San Francisco as to go all the way to Tokyo – I NEED YOUR POWER, LORD"! Heaven came down and glory filled my soul with Joy and Love unspeakable – and the Lord baptized me in His Holy Spirit, with a New Power! Suddenly, in His Sovereign Majesty, with no one present, the Lord changed my life *totally*! After that, everything seemed to be done *through me* in a way I had never before experienced! In the middle of the ocean, an effective Vacation Bible School was miraculously set up for the children – but it was done effortlessly! The experience of the Baptism in the Holy Spirit was totally unexpected because I had thought that it was only for the early Christian Church. Yet, God began to give me words of wisdom, knowledge and discerning of spirits to counsel many of the wives who were worried about rejoining their husbands because of the fear that they had been "shacked up with Japanese women" during the long months (or years) they were away from home. Some of them gratefully said to me as I left the ship that I had "become the Lady Chaplain". To God be the Glory!

We disembarked in Yokohama and were overjoyed to be met by my husband who took us to a lovely Japanese resort hotel in the mountains. Everything was *so* different: small trees and beautiful rock gardens; sleeping on futons or sitting on square flat pillows or woven tatami instead of chairs and rugs or carpets. Sounds and smells were so different from home and it made us know that we were in an entirely different culture with a new and unknown language and people with slanted eyes, wearing kimonos and thong sandals who came smilingly to wait on us and make us comfortable! After that idyllic weekend, we drove to the American quarters in Tokyo and I almost fainted for there was the Japanese maid, standing at the door, waiting to carry in the bags – just exactly as the Lord had prophesied to me sixteen months before on that momentous afternoon in Norfolk! She turned out to be a wonderful housekeeper who loved the children and cooked all our meals and cheerfully cleaned the house every day.

Sachiko-san had gone to a Mission School as a little girl; but during the war, she had married a "kamikaze pilot" who lost his life in a suicidal dive bombing of one of our ships. She came to work for American Naval families because she wanted to improve her English and educate their daughter to be a lawyer. One of my husband's friends who was moving back to the States, kindly released Sachiko-san two weeks early – so that she could come to work for me on my arrival in Japan. As the months went by, in sharing with her my faith in Jesus, I found that she had lost her Christian faith and was praying to her dead husband! What a joy it was to see her return to her earlier faith. She was always smiling and nothing was too hard for her to do for our family! The Buddhist religion cripples people with fear. She had found the joy of the Lord!

After a few weeks, our limited belongings were in place in our government furnished quarters and the children had been entered in the US Navy-run School. I had been impatiently praying for the Lord to lead me to the missionary work He had called me to do. One morning, He told me to brave the very real hazards of driving in Tokyo and go to a certain area of that largest city in the world – and there I would find a building with a cross on it! My heart beat rapidly as in my large Buick sedan, I managed to avoid bicycles and taxis that swerved towards me unexpectedly – some bicycle riders carrying tall stacks of bowls of noodles in one hand which they balanced precariously as they wove in and out of traffic. There were swarms of miniature cars, jitneys, trucks and hordes of pedestrians! Just as I found what I suddenly knew in my heart was "the right building with the cross on it", I looked at my watch in dismay. It was time to go home and join my husband for lunch! So the next morning I set out again with the Lord's Presence giving me a sense of peace and purposefulness. This time I was ushered into the office of a short, intelligent, respected Japanese Anglican priest. The Harvard University pennant hanging on the wall caught my immediate attention as I am a Wellesley College graduate. I suddenly remembered many happy times when I had dated Harvard students while I was an undergraduate at Wellesley! The Lord confirmed in the ensuing conversation that *here* was my call!

Dr. Enkichi Kan and his wife (a Yale University graduate) had been praying for the Lord to send a Christian who would teach the Bible for the first time in Nihon Joshi Dai, the leading Woman's University in Tokyo where Mrs. Kan was a Department head. The person who had to cancel her teaching commitment there because of sudden illness was a Wellesley graduate – so I was God's substitute! I was allowed to teach the Bible because the Dean so much wanted an American to teach English to their Juniors and Seniors who had never had English-speaking teachers. When I stated that I would need to teach the Bible, as well as English, they granted me permission to teach "where it had never been taught before" – just as the Lord had promised back in Norfolk seventeen months previously! It was such a joy to teach *Ephesians* and the *Gospels* to my four classes – to help them learn not just the English language but, more importantly, to study God's Word! My students found the Love of Jesus – and they studied nine hours in preparation for each of my classes. They memorized verses, paraphrased paragraphs, sang Christian songs – and when we had to return to the States a year later, 28 of them came the long journey (by train and on foot) to Yokohama carrying armloads of exotic flowers and gifts of beautiful furoshike. The flowers filled our cabin and even the tub – and overflowed to the ship's dining room. The blossoms in a few days faded and the beautiful silk scarves have long since deteriorated – but one unusual lacquered tray still reminds me of their love – for on it are engraved in impressive Chinese characters: "God's Love Never Fails"! Chinese characters are considered more elite than Japanese ones.

Truly, the Lord had kept *His* promise and given me *His* Love for the Japanese people! I had traveled twice a week on crowded trains where the Japanese men's hair tonic almost asphyxiated me as they were shorter than I. I had to take two taxis and three different trains to travel from my home to the University – each way – on the days I taught classes. Grading their papers was a formidable chore because they had not had good English teachers and were only at about 8th grade level by American standards. But many of them came to the Lord and their minds were opened to the Truth of God's Word. In Buddhism (a pagan religion) there is so much fear: their idea of heaven, "nirvana", is perpetual nothingness! One could easily spot the Christians because of the Light and Joy in their faces.

God is so good – He keeps His promises! He taught me to teach them – and the lessons that I wrote to use in my classes became chapters in my first book, *THE TRANSFORMING POWER OF GOD.* I had prayed constantly: "Teach me, Lord, that I may teach" – and He did. Later, Dr. Kan asked my permission to translate these chapters into Japanese, saying: "This is just what our Japanese students have needed." Praise God! That year, Dr. Kan was trying to re-open a Seminary that had been closed during World War II. Dick and I were able to contribute some substantial funds to help; and the royalties from *THE TRANSFORMING POWER OF GOD* (later published in the States) went to promote that worthy cause. Again, God's Promise was fulfilled! I was amazed how each detail came true – and it strengthened my faith to see *His* faithfulness to *His* Promises. I *only needed to be faithful and obedient to Him*!

It was awesome to see how He was transforming my life! I was being given courage to stand up for what I knew was the Lord's Will – even in spite of opposition that would have previously silenced me. Minutes seemed to be stretched so that each day was amazingly productive. That year I felt as if I were living three lives at once! As a high ranking Naval Officer's wife on an Admiral's staff, I had many official duties – but often the Admiral's wife would excuse me saying, "What you are doing is more important" or "I wish I had your faith". The Lord impressed on Dick and me that I was not to take a salary for my teaching but rather to set up a "Scholarship Fund" since it would hurt the Dean's pride not to pay me a salary. This was something unheard of in Japan. Later in the year, a student was able to continue her University training after her father died suddenly, leaving her without funds. I prayed that the word "sensei" (teacher) would take on new meaning – that my students would see Jesus, the Teacher, as the One who loved them – not their concept of teachers to be feared, as was their custom. But one day they taught me something when they asked: "But, if you Christians *love* each other, how is it that we have to become Presbyterian Christians or Methodist Christians or Baptist Christians, or Anglican (Episcopalian) Christians or Roman Catholic Christians? Why can't you get along with each other?" I pondered that in my heart.

So, I prayed that the healing ministry into which the Lord was leading me would become an ecumenical one. And so it has! Victorious Ministry Through Christ, which my husband and I founded eighteen years later in Florida, now has a Board of Directors of two Episcopalian priests, two Methodist pastors, two Presbyterians, two Lutherans, two Independent Charismatic pastors and one Disciples of Christ minister. We minister together lovingly – not judgmentally – to one another (as well as to clergy and lay people from these and other denominations) because VMTC is empowered by the Holy Spirit, based on the authority of God's Word and the Victory of Calvary. To Him be the Glory!

The true sign of the Baptism in the Holy Spirit is a *changed life*! Peter, who wrote the stirring Epistles and was martyred for his faith, was not the same Peter after Pentecost as the fisherman-disciple who had denied knowing his Lord! In my own case, I was so changed that I had to get to know the "new me". Also, I had to study God's Word carefully because I had once taught that this life-changing experience was only for one dispensation! Yet here I, the formerly timid one, was so changed that people have come to say: "When the Lord healed Anne of her shyness, He did too good a job!" I could underline even today in my first book the things that I wrote from an intellectual knowledge – but the most important words came from the Holy Spirit! The wisdom to know how to counsel others was the outworking of the supernatural gifts of "wisdom, knowledge, discerning of spirits and faith" because I had never had any secular training to be a counselor! The "gifts of healings" were being given through my prayers to those in need in an Army Hospital where I served each week as a "Gray Lady" – and came back the next week to see the Lord's miracles that had taken place! It was an awesome year!

The Lord kept opening up more opportunities to teach the Bible through "the back-door of teaching English". I had a class in the Dean's Office of Rikkyo Daigaku, the leading Anglican University. I also taught classes one day each week in the Boys' Primary School which was connected with this major missionary project. Because my daughter was in 8th grade, I taught English to a Junior High School class. It was challenging to keep up with the Holy Spirit! When I supplied the willingness, He supplied the Power!

I did not at once receive the "gift of tongues" – but all of the other supernatural gifts (manifestations) were clearly operating, including "prophecy". I did not realize the true significance of the things that I was writing down at the Lord's prompting until some years later when they came true! Twenty of those that I had saved became the first prophecies identified as such by Rev. Canon Michael Harper when I lived in England in 1964 – and they were published (at his urging) with later ones given to me by the Lord in my book, *DAYSPRING*. I had received the Baptism in the Holy Spirit in 1953 aboard the transport crossing the Pacific. While we were en route, the Korean War Armistice was proclaimed! I heard loud shouts from the hundreds of servicemen aboard the transport – and I knew from the Lord (not from men) the cause of their joy! What a tremendous relief to know that the War had ended!

When we returned home in August 1954, I heard for the first time of Dennis Bennett's experience. My previous brief contact with a rather noisy group of Pentecostals had so prejudiced me against "tongues speaking" that the Lord did not give me that particular gift until some years later when I was earnestly interceding for a young man and said: "Lord use my faith, my tongue, *use all of me* to heal him!" The lady next to me later commented: "Did you know that you were "praying in tongues"? Prejudice against any of God's gifts can block us from receiving His blessings. We need to accept the authority of God's Word without prejudice. As James' Epistle tells us, He is the Giver of *good gifts !*

We need to know beyond a shadow of a doubt that *all* His gifts are *good* and needed in our ministry! When we ask to receive the Baptism in the Holy Spirit, we need to repent of any previous prejudices or doubts (either our own or our parents' influence on us) and begin to thank and praise God that He will entrust us with His overcoming Power. Losing ourselves in deep intercessory prayer for others is a way that God can use – if our intellects are standing in the way of our receiving this blessing. I can now say with Paul: "I pray in tongues more than you all." In fact, when I'm traveling, I find it very helpful to pray in tongues; and the rougher the weather, the more valuable is my "prayer language"! God has blessed me with a "praise language" – and when I hear that, I rejoice all the more at His Victory being won in spiritual warfare. When we do not know how God wants us to pray, we can (as Scripture says) intercede with groanings and utterings that we do not understand. *(Romans 8:26)* The Holy Spirit is then praying *through* us.

Our intellects can still understand if we ask for the gift of "interpretation of tongues". We must choose to accept all of God's gifts as good gifts!

Once we were praying for a man to receive that particular gift and he was blocking the Lord's Purposes with his unbelief. We asked him to pray in his new prayer language – and then receive the interpretation from the Lord. Reluctantly, he spoke one word "come" – and we encouraged him to let the Lord use his voice further. Hesitantly, he added "over the hill" – and then he became frustrated and said that this was foolishness! We urged him to repeat those four words and continue to speak – and out of his mouth came: "Come over the hill of doubt!" Why do earnest Christians doubt the validity of God's supernatural gifts when they are needed for the building up of the Church? In Africa and other places, it is far easier for people to receive their prayer language than in this country. Could it be that our pride of intellect can cut us off from receiving all of God's gifts? Has the argument in so many Churches (as to whether we need gifts or fruit of the Spirit) been the work of the enemy? The fact is that Christians need both! Gifts can be given in an instant but fruit takes time to grow! My orange tree never says: "Oomph" and produces an orange! It takes almost a year from the time I smell the sweet fragrance of a blossom until the time I can pick the juicy orange fruit from my tree! As you and I abide in Christ, we will bear much fruit (we are told in John 15:5). The orange tree does not strain to produce fruit because the branch is connected to the trunk – not cut off from its source of supply. Neither will we bear fruit if we are not connected to Jesus. It is our day by day abiding in Him that enables us to bear fruit – in spite of the enemy's slandering, discouraging, nagging voice that often tries to keep us from maturing in the Lord.

We need the gifts to empower us in ministry – else we will be guilty of trying to do things on our own, instead of giving ourselves over to Jesus to be used by the Holy Spirit to accomplish His Purposes for our lives. We need to covet the *highest* gifts – those real manifestations of the Holy Spirit – not to seek psychic powers with which Satan will tempt us. Paul cast out the spirit of divination, the psychic power, that was controlling the slave girl – and then she could no longer tell the fortunes, a money-making power for her owners – but obviously not a gift of the Holy Spirit! *(Acts 16: 16-18)* Christians today should ask God's forgiveness for any dabbling they have done in occult practices – even though they might not have been aware of this sin of seeking wisdom other than from the Lord or using psychic powers. Then, after receiving His forgiveness, they should renounce any and all psychic contacts or powers or experiences – before asking Him to empower them with His supernatural gifts. The Church desperately needs the empowering of the Holy Spirit today!

When listening to others, we can pray silently in the Spirit and hear with our intellects. We can drive our cars with our intellects and pray (or sing) in the Spirit – and we will most probably have fewer accidents. God is yearning to equip His obedient children who are willing to humble themselves and let Him empower their lives with His gifts. Praying in the Spirit can clear our minds of negative, fearful thoughts. Our faith is in Jesus, the Baptizer in the Spirit, who has not only saved us but also *wants to equip and empower us to carry on His ministry*! When He came to the disciples on Easter night as they huddled in fear in the Upper Room in Jerusalem, Jesus breathed on them and said: "Receive the Holy Spirit". *(John 20:22)* But the author of Luke's Gospel quoted Jesus as saying later to those same disciples: "but you shall receive power when the Holy

Spirit has come upon you; and you shall be My witnesses both in Jerusalem, and in all Judea and Samaria, and even to the remotest part of the earth." *(Acts 1:8)* Obviously, they needed the second blessing of Pentecost when they became fully empowered by the Holy Spirit to preach and teach and heal the sick – fearlessly in the Name of Jesus – regardless of the threats of the authorities who tried in every way to silence them and their compelling witness to the Resurrection. Many were martyred for their faith and went to their deaths singing hymns of joy! In some countries Christians are persecuted today.

When several years later the Lord gave me the gift of "interpretation of tongues", the person who was praying for me wrote in red ink the Lord's words of interpretation: "Go into all the world and preach the Gospel in My Love – and fear not any man". Out of obedience to Jesus' call, I have made ten trips of ministry around the world; eighteen to Australia; many to Pakistan, Singapore and New Zealand with side trips to Malaysia, Indonesia, the Philippines and Sabah – as well as many to England, Sweden, Norway and Denmark and two to Kenya. Without this commissioning and the empowering of the Holy Spirit, I could not have fulfilled Jesus' call! God is no respecter of persons – but of conditions. *He can and will use any of us if we will submit our wills to His Will* – not our own! For some of us, He may be saying: "Bloom where you are planted". Fruit is grown in the valleys – not on the mountain tops. We do not have to run around seeking our ministry. He will guide us and unfold it, opening the necessary doors when we are ready to walk through them *obedient to His Will*, rather than trying to do our own thing! Are you ready to make that *total* commitment and receive the empowering of His Holy Spirit? It may mean giving up something (or someone) you idolize. It may mean forgiving someone you don't want to forgive – or loving someone you don't want to love. That secret sin you don't want to give up may be an idol. We are clearly warned in *James' Epistle 1:7-8* that double-mindedness can be a barrier to total commitment. It means to lay aside our preconceived opinions and believe in God's mighty Power by faith. It also means that our surrender to Jesus is total and our acceptance of our place with Him makes us ready to follow Him at all costs. Satan can oppress Christians in areas of their lives that they have not given over to the control of the Holy Spirit. Our eyes need to be singly fixed on Jesus – and *then His Light in us can overcome the darkness of spiritual warfare.* Jesus has called us all to be overcomers – in His Wisdom and Strength to overcome evil with good! In *John 16:33*, Jesus promises to us as well as to those disciples: "In the world you have tribulation but take courage; I have overcome the world". To God be the Glory!

WINNING VICTORY IN SPIRITUAL WARFARE

CHAPTER IV

FROM JAPAN TO EUROPE

When we returned home from Japan in August of 1954, I heard of others who had also experienced the "Baptism in the Holy Spirit" – but we were a very small group! For me, always "preaching the kingdom and healing the sick" were linked together – whether in a formal service or in a time of prayer and/or counseling with the sick. Teaching (whether spoken or in writing) was really a matter of my surrendering my mind and heart and voice to the Lord so that He could speak through me! I became active in the healing ministry of several churches in Texas – and a year later in Virginia, when we moved back to Norfolk. Some months afterwards, twenty doctors on the Tumor Board at the large Naval Hospital in Portsmouth, VA, diagnosed a malignant tumor on our son's thyroid gland. On Sunday, after the Communion Service, our Rector anointed Richard with oil, and thus began the first healing service at our Church. Richard had served as an acolyte and we were all expecting God's miracle. However, a few days later, when the doctors operated on him, they found it necessary to remove not only the egg-sized tumor, but also three-quarters of his thyroid gland! We were assured that Richard could be given adequate thyroid supplements – but to the doctors' amazement, he never needed them! He recovered very quickly from this most delicate operation. Every month the doctors insisted on checking his condition, as he was only thirteen years old, and they thought that this was a temporary remission. Finally, after five years, tests were made which confirmed the fact that the one-quarter of his thyroid gland had grown into the necessary perfect half! Thanks be to God for His miracle of restoration and healing!

Before we moved from Norfolk, Virginia to England in 1961, I led Weekend Healing Missions in a few churches. Dick and I had prayed for the Lord to guide us to his next duty station, and the word came clearly to us both – "London"! I had surrendered our lovely home (the nicest we had ever owned) to the Lord – and He took it! So, for the next three years, we lived in a large furnished "flat" – the second floor of a mansion, overlooking a wind-swept park. To heat this new home, we had a large electric heater that put out a great deal of light, but little heat; a coal grate in one fire place, and a gas grill in another. We had to use small electric heaters in each bedroom, and the 'Aladdin' heater in the kitchen was in constant use, along with the oven to help us survive the coldest winter they had had in sixty-five years! Dick loved England and we traveled extensively.

Living in London enabled me to be involved in the work of two of their Healing Missions, and in services at Holy Trinity Church in Brompton Road. In God's timing, a door opened for me to co-lead in Sweden a "Christian Ashram" with Dr. E. Stanley Jones, the well-known Methodist missionary to India. But, as he had to cancel unexpectedly, the Lord empowered me to lead the Weekend Retreat in his place – much to my amazement! I had learned from Dr. Jones something that has changed my life: "When you supply the willingness, God will supply the power!" This led to further "Ashram" Retreats leadership in Norway, Denmark and England – and later in the USA after we returned home. In 1970 and 1971, I led the seminar on healing for clergy and their wives at the Eatonton, GA. "CFO" – but their curfew and other schedule limitations prevented the four-hour counseling sessions needed for this in-depth ministry to be effective. Clergy working with us realized that this specialized work of the Holy Spirit could no longer be an incidental part of some other type of ministry, but needed to become in itself a "para-Church" ministry – known as "Victorious Ministry Through Christ". So, on January 13, 1971, Dick and I were led to incorporate the ministry in the State of Florida on a firm legal foundation of its own. I have never taken a salary or any income from my books or speaking engagements. Financial gifts from many other thankful people and churches have also helped to support this growing ministry.

Doing VMTC Prayer Ministry in each country, our trained, Spirit-filled ministers have seen over and over again wonderful healings of broken marriages and parent/child relationships. Lives of those receiving this ministry have been so transformed that often they have later made a serious commitment to be trained in VMTC Schools so that God could use them to bring His blessings to others. Drug addicts and homosexuals have been released to lead Spirit-filled lives, after having been healed and baptized in the Holy Spirit with power to overcome their past problems. Many types of physical healings have also resulted from this Scriptural, balanced, effective ministry of the Holy Spirit through those who have themselves received the ministry and been trained in VMTC's Clergy Schools of Prayer Ministry – in order to keep the "creative conformity" of this vital work of the Holy Spirit. The basic Team consists of a man and a woman carefully trained in our Schools.

VMTC Prayer Ministry has never been "inner healing". It is not "creative imagination therapy" or "healing of the memories" or "visualization". Instead of "creative imagination therapy", in our ecumenical ministry, VMTC stresses only "creative conformity" to the principles of prayer set forth in the Word of God. Instead of using imagination, which is unreality, we stress the need to use "the Sword of the Spirit" to bring the healing reality of Jesus' freedom from many life-long relationship bondages and oppressing spirits in order "to set the captives free". Scripture speaks of "casting down vain imaginations" – not creating them. God's Word tells us that He "heals the broken hearted and binds up their wounds". *(Psalms 147:3)* There is no reference in the Word to the "healing of memories" or "inner healing". It does say: "The inward thoughts of the mind and heart are deep" *(Psalms 64:6)* but that is a description of what the medical profession calls the deep "subconscious mind" today. Episcopal clergy, in pronouncing absolution, have for years said: "pardon and deliver". The Lord's prayer says "Deliver us from evil". In *Luke 9:1-2*, we read Jesus' twin commands: "preach the kingdom and heal the sick" – so VMTC ministry calls us not only to repentance and forgiveness as an essential avenue of healing but also to commit our lives more fully to Jesus Christ! VMTC is a ministry that brings freedom and wholeness so that we can make (and keep) a deeper commitment. A commitment ministry is not just to solve problems, but to change people who need the healing of relationships in order to be made whole!

Another of the differences between VMTC Prayer Ministry and some of these others, is that ours has always been initiated and carried out under appropriate, responsible Church authority – not only in the USA, but also in each of the many countries where it has been established. From the very beginning, the Lord guided my husband and me to place my God-given healing ministry not only under his authority, but also that of our Church. I have always been authorized by my Rector and my Bishop for this traveling ministry which has become progressively more extensive!

From the very beginning, Dick and I made sure that my ministry was under the authority of the Bishop of the Diocese of Central Florida – at first it was Bishop William H. Folwell (who encouraged my lay ministry) and in recent years, Bishop John W. Howe (who is a most anointed, Spirit-filled, Scriptural teacher). During many years when he was my rector, I was blessed by the active encouragement of Rev. Donis Patterson until he moved away to become Bishop of Dallas (now retired). Annually, I make a detailed report to the Bishop on my lay ministry in order to maintain this authority and to be covered by his prayers. The letter I receive in response is my "spiritual driver's license"– and I carry it in my wallet along with a list of the members of the VMTC Board of Directors and Advisory Council. Being under authority is a blessing!

In December, 1970, a very small "pilot school" in Florida prepared the way for the first Clergy School of Prayer Ministry held the next month in Atlanta, Georgia. On January 13, 1971, Victorious Ministry Through Christ was legally established as a non-profit, religious, educational corporation in the State of Florida to receive all income from my books, honoraria and missions – so that Clergy Schools of Prayer Ministry could be held wherever needed in various parts of the USA and abroad. This financial undergirding over the years has paid for the transportation, accommodations and meals of team members (averaging about 10) for each U.S. Clergy School. None of the team members receive remuneration. At Dick's request, the first Board of Directors consisted of two Presbyterian pastors, one Episcopal priest, my husband (as Vice-President and Treasurer) and myself as President. Initially, two key lay women on the Board (as counselors) helped the three clergy and me in training others at the Schools – four being held in West Virginia, North Carolina, Florida and Georgia. From this early beginning, VMTC ministry has, by God's provision, expanded across the USA – so that for many years (with the magnificent help of our clergy Board of Directors and lay teams) I have coordinated the Clergy Schools of Prayer Ministry from Florida to New Jersey and across the country to Tennessee, Michigan, Illinois, New Mexico and California. Thus, cumulatively, many thousands of clergy and lay people have received the blessing of being healed – set free from their bondages to people, places, experiences and things – and from the results of their own sins of alienation from others as well as, often, from themselves and from God! Their wounds have been healed by the Lord Jesus in a strictly Scriptural, balanced and effective ministry – based on the authority of God's Word, claiming specifically the Victory of Calvary – in the power and through the gifts of the Holy Spirit! The Lord led me over several formative years in the early 60's to develop a specific Scriptural, balanced pattern of prayer called "VMTC Prayer Counseling". In the 70's and 80's He led me "to give the ministry to the Church" as VMTC Schools trained clergy and lay people to minister in their local congregations. In 1994, our Board of Directors was led by the Holy Spirit to change the name to "Prayer Ministry" to avoid confusion with those who also use the words "Prayer Counseling" – but have different standards. With the approval of their wives and Churches, those pastors have traveled with me in the overseas "travelogue" which followed. Over the past 27 years, the Lord has opened doors successively in an amazing fashion! *DAYSPRING*, a collection of many prophecies with Scriptural bases, years ago had foretold this international ministry which has involved ten trips around the world and eighteen to Australia – a total of over 30 countries where I have ministered as God unfolded His Plan!

Simultaneously with this initial growth of my ministry in the USA, the Lord opened doors for me in England – building on the fact that my second book, *HEALING ADVENTURE*, was first published there in 1969. Also, the clergy contacts made during our three year Navy tour of duty were helpful. I had attended their first "Conference on the Holy Spirit" and other meetings sponsored by the Rev. Canon Michael Harper. It was no accident that the itinerary planned by him as a result of reading my new book included speaking at three of his Fountain Trust Conferences, as well as leading Seminars for clergy and parish workers. I led many Weekend Missions on the "Healing of Relationships" in Methodist, Baptist, Anglican and Congregational Churches – with the "laying-on of hands" ministry concluding each service. Returning in the Spring of 1971 at his invitation, I spoke at a major conference where Michael Harper had asked me to lead a group of about 60 clergy and their wives in the basic teaching of VMTC Prayer Ministry – with a team being trained between the larger meetings. In 1972, this led to the establishment of the first two Clergy Schools of Prayer Ministry co-led by me with a small American team and these key English clergy and their wives. In the next two years, the ministry became established under the leadership of the Board of Directors of VMTC-Great Britain, and I became a member of their Trust.

At the same time that our American clergy and lay teams were helping me set up training Schools in England, I was traveling to Sweden to lead Retreats and Teaching Missions in churches near Stockholm. The Lord had also opened this door for a deeper work in the Spirit because of my previous ministry in the early 60's in Sweden. Now, I was being called by Him to set up the Clergy Schools of Prayer Ministry with their Lutheran State and "Free" Church leadership. *HEALING ADVENTURE* was translated by the pastor of the largest "Free Church" in Stockholm and was published by the Methodist Publishing House there – and later my books *DAYSPRING* and *TRIAL BY FIRE* followed. This was a significant aspect of charismatic renewal in Sweden.

With the help of two of our American Clergy Board members and a few lay people, we trained Swedish leadership. In 1980, their work met with the standards the Lord had given us – so that VMTC-Sweden was set up under their ecumenical Board of Directors. During this time, a few Finnish pastors and lay people called for our help as they saw the need in Finland for the Lord's blessing through VMTC Prayer Ministry. With the help of some Swedish Board members, the Clergy Schools of Prayer Ministry were set up near Helsinki – after the Lord had used me to lay the groundwork through leading VMTC Retreats and Missions at the invitation of Finnish State Church and Pentecostal clergy. *HEALING ADVENTURE* was translated into Finnish – after VMTC-Finland was officially set up in 1980 – having met our International Standards for this ministry. We joyously presided over the signing of the International Covenant Agreement with Finland's VMTC Board of Directors. (See *JESUS, ALL IN ALL*, pp. 94-96 for a crisis overcome).

Our VMTC International Teaching Outlines and approved prayer ministry procedures have been translated into Swedish and Finnish so that the "creative conformity" that the Lord had clearly impressed on us could be maintained. In Sweden, the ministry grew much stronger after they began to hold VMTC Training Schools in their own language. In Finland, their difficulties were greater as they have both Swedish and Finnish speaking churches. In 1985, I led a VMTC Retreat in Norway and a Teaching Mission followed in a lovely Lutheran Church. Two years later, a U.S. Board member and I spoke in several churches in Stockholm and Upsala before attending the Nordic Countries' Conference chaired by the President of VMTC-Finland with the help of the Swedish Vice-President of "Helhet Genom Kristus". It was agreed there that under this joint leadership, VMTC Prayer Ministry Schools could begin the training of Norwegian clergy and lay people. Later, I returned to Norway to approve of their work – and one of their key leadership clergy couples attended a U.S. School to be sure that they were keeping the "creative conformity" which the Lord had shown us was very important for this international work of the Spirit. It was challenging in some European Schools to have three languages being used in a ministry session! On one occasion, the other team member (who spoke fluently the three languages) stopped the dialogue to interpret for me what had been said – but I already knew, as the Holy Spirit had revealed to me the gist of the situation. The gift of interpretation of tongues was especially needed!

Often people have asked me what super-vitamin I take, and my reply is: *Philippians 4:13.* "The joy of the Lord is my strength" is a favorite verse. (*Nehemiah 8:10*) In times of intense spiritual warfare, when the enemy attacks with spirits of "helplessness and hopelessness," I lean on the promises: "The

Lord God is my strength, my personal bravery and my invincible army; He makes my feet like hinds' feet, and will make me to walk [not to stand still in terror, but to walk] and make [spiritual] progress upon my high places [of trouble, suffering and responsibility]." *Habakkuk 3:19 (Ampl.)*

When we are undergoing our many trials by fire, we need to claim with faith the important promise: "Thanks be to God who gives us the victory through our Lord Jesus Christ"! (*I Corinthians 15:57*). To God be the Glory!

CHAPTER V

GOING HOME TO THE LORD

It was 12:30 at night in March, 1966 when we reached the Army Hospital on the far side of Atlanta and my husband was admitted to the Intensive Care Unit as he was suffering from a massive coronary! His Executive Officer, our neighbor, had hastily dressed to drive us to the hospital as Dick was in such agony I knew that I could not drive him that long distance alone. Unbeknownst to me, the Executive Officer had telephoned the Navy Department in Washington, D.C. to pass on the news that the doctors who admitted Dick to the hospital did not expect him to live through the night. Because "death benefits" would be better for my future pension, the Judge Advocate General's office had put through Dick's "retirement from active duty" papers – as of the time he was admitted to the hospital – although I was not told of this till days later!

I was thankful that the head nurse allowed me to sit in the room with him where I could quietly pray as they carried out their procedures. I was praying for the Lord to send spiritual reinforcements as I had not had time to call "prayer warrior" friends before we left home. When at 4:00AM the door opened and a young Baptist Chaplain

51

quietly asked me about our Church affiliation, I knew that the Lord had answered that prayer. To my dismay, he started to go out the door – but I asked him to come back and pray for Dick – which he did. Gently touching my husband, the Chaplain prayed: "Thank you, Father, that You are healing this Your son, according to Your perfect Plan" – and he quietly left the room. I could sense at once that God was answering that prayer – and the next day Dick confirmed the miracle of divine healing by surprising the doctors as he showed *real* signs of recovery! A few days later, another Chaplain visited Dick and I asked him to pray. To my horror, he began gloomily to pray: "Oh Lord, let this Thy poor suffering servant find some measure of comfort" – and I watched my husband's face turn gray as if he were about to have another heart attack! So, I quickly ushered this Chaplain out of the room saying that I didn't think my husband could take any more. Because it was such a negative response, I did not mention it to Dick for several days – and when I did, he replied that he was angry that a man of God was preaching a funeral sermon over him when he was fighting for his life! We praised the Lord together for Dick's healing which continued until he was able to return home. He was so thankful to be home that as he came in the kitchen door, he almost hugged the refrigerator! This healing brought him into a very close relationship with Jesus. Dick had always been generous in giving; he was for many years regular in his church attendance; and he had been a licensed Lay Reader in the Episcopal Church in three states as well as in the Anglican Church which we attended in London during our three-year tour of duty there. But it was so different to see him call on the Name of Jesus whenever angina pains returned. The

Lord told Dick that He had saved his life to cover my ministry!

My husband's recovery was so steady and fast that he soon began to plan what he would do as the Navy had retired him early (in 1966) on the basis of this service-incurred disability. We prayed for guidance and he felt that he was to take a Masters-in-Teaching degree at the University and embark on a second career. Soon after beginning this intensive course where he was competing with much younger men, Dick began to show signs of over-stress. In a different way, he was repeating the old patterns of stress reaction to enormous pressure that had caused the first heart attack six months before. To our dismay, one day we had to rush him to the same Army Hospital as he was suffering from another coronary! This physical set-back was a shock to his faith – and, although we prayed again for God's healing Touch, Dick found it harder to believe for another miracle. About that time, an Episcopal Church in Atlanta was holding a Healing Mission. As I knew that the Missioner was both an Episcopal priest and a medical doctor, I begged him to come to the hospital to pray with Dick. Dr. Bill Beachy graciously left his busy schedule to make this visit and the Lord led him to ask Dick a very significant question: "Captain White, you have had a distinguished career in the Navy. What are you trying to prove?" The Lord used those words to convict Dick that he did not need to go back to such a stressful life style as he had planned. Again, Jesus made Himself more real than ever before – and Dick accepted the reality of retirement.

Living in Atlanta presented problems as the climate was too cold in the winter and the terrain was too hilly for

Dick to follow his usual health program of walking two miles a day. Furthermore, we were living in a townhouse and the stairs were too much for his heart. We prayed for guidance and the doctor urged us to move to Florida. Dick was 80% disabled at the time when he was released from the hospital – but during the next eight years, his healing continued so that he was able to offer his services to the Red Cross and also to a local Church School that needed his accounting skills. Truly, we had the best eight years of our marriage!

We drove down in January '67 and fell in love with Winter Park, where we bought a home. We had been led to a Church with a healing ministry. Within a few months, I became actively a part of the healing ministry at two of our Church's weekly Healing Services. The Lord brought about a gradual healing that enabled Dick to become our Church's Treasurer and a very committed, active vestry-man. The clergy often said that Dick ministered to them! As previously mentioned, Dick and I founded Victorious Ministry Through Christ on January 13, 1971 in thanks-giving to the Lord for His healing power. VMTC was set up as a non-profit, religious, educational corporation to receive all income from my books, Conference honoraria and Teaching Missions – for the support of Clergy Schools of Prayer Ministry which have now been held in various areas of the USA as well as in eight countries around the world.

A few years later, we followed the Lord's guidance when He told us to take a certain tour of the Holy Land. While there, on the Sea of Galilee, a minister prayed for Dick during a special healing service – and again he experienced the Lord's Touch in a miraculous way! Everyone could see the difference – especially after he received the Baptism in the Holy Spirit in an upper room in a Jerusalem Hotel! Dick's mother was elderly and needed his daily loving attention – so he could not travel with me – but he released me with his blessing for eleven days each month as the VMTC Schools and Weekend Teaching Missions spread from Florida to other states. His wisdom and prayer covering were very important as well as his work as VMTC's Treasurer and Vice-President. His commitment was a great blessing to me!

In 1973, our daughter had come from Scotland to visit us for Christmas and they had experienced a needed and meaningful reconciliation after some long-standing hurts were at last resolved. (These were the results of the Navy life with its necessarily long absences during the War – and later, when Dick was away from home on duty in Japan for over a year.) Also, VMTC had been experiencing a serious problem in its leadership which brought very heavy emotional pressure on Dick – and which we later realized was a result of spiritual warfare. One Sunday morning, as I was dressing to go to Church to speak on healing at the Coffee Hour, Dick told me good-bye as he went out the back door saying: "I'll meet you at Church for the later service – and I will be praying for you while you are giving your talk on healing there." I thought that he was off for his usual two mile walk, still a necessary part of his health program. Instead, he had decided to surprise me by riding his old English bicycle (which he had had repaired, unbeknownst to me). To my horror, about twenty minutes later, a neighbor banged frantically on our back door saying: "Call the ambulance! Dick has collapsed under his bicycle in the little park at the top of the hill!" I was unable to get the Ambulance – and by the time the Rescue Squad arrived at the scene, I could see that the paramedic corpsmen were very agitated as they bent over Dick's still body. The trip to the nearest hospital took longer than usual as the driver started out the wrong way. When Dick was admitted to the Intensive Care Unit, the doctors were very concerned about his condition and did not expect him to live through the night! He was in a coma. Our son and daughter-in-law flew in from Chicago – a real miracle to get a flight through Atlanta Airport! Dick was not responding in any way – and in fact, he never spoke or showed any sign of recognition. For nineteen long days, he lingered in a coma – each morning's EEG tests showing that the brain damage had increased. One of our VMTC Board Members prayed and got the word, "Release". Several clergy from two Churches, including our Bishop, came to pray for him. I could only turn him over to the Lord as the doctor's verdict was that Dick would be a "vegetable" if he ever came out of the coma. To me, "living death" was not God's will for my husband – nor would it have been Dick's – if he could have spoken for himself! One afternoon, some of us prayed very earnestly to release him to the Lord – and I was blessed when He gave me for Dick, the Scripture in *II Timothy 4:7-8*: "I have fought the good fight, I have finished the course, I have kept the faith; in the future there is laid up for me the crown of righteousness, which the Lord, the righteous Judge, will award to me on that day; *and not only to me, but also to all who have loved His appearing.*" (Italics mine)

In the fullness of His Love, I knew that God was telling me gently that He was going "to call Dick Home" as he had "fought the good fight, finished the course and kept the faith." God was promising "the crown of righteousness" as Dick was a committed Spirit-filled servant who loved Jesus. After awhile, I was led to ask the Lord: "What about me?" And again He turned my eyes to the Scripture in *II Timothy 4:5*, "But you, be sober in all things, endure hardship, do the work of an evangelist, fulfill your ministry." God's Peace came over me for the first time since the accident – and I went home from the hospital with a new sense of His comfort and strength. At 1:00AM, the doctor called me to say that Dick had just breathed his last breath. My response was: "Thank you, doctor, for your care. I know that he has 'gone Home to the Lord'"! It was such a relief for me to know that Dick was now in the Nearer Presence of Jesus and would spend his days praising the Lord at the Throne of Grace – instead of being shut up in the "incurable area" of a nursing home in what to me would have been "living death".

Suddenly, I knew why in the past on three occasions, I had had a strange experience of Jesus' Presence as I returned to my pew from the altar rail of our Church after receiving Holy Communion. Three times I had heard very clearly within me: "Thou art the Bride of Christ." I had responded: "Yes, I know I am a member of the Church, the Bride of Christ." But now I *knew* that the Lord had been quietly preparing my heart for an even deeper commitment to Him – that I would not re-marry but give my life totally to Jesus. Words of Scripture came back to me: the promise that He would be the "husband to the widow" and that He would never leave me comfortless! (*Isaiah 54:5; Jeremiah 49:11*)

It had been agreed that our daughter would return home from Scotland later during her Easter holiday. Our son and daughter-in-law flew down again and we had a meaningful, quiet service in our beautiful Church – just as Dick would have wanted it. It was truly a joyous Resurrection Service – for we knew that he had "gone Home to the Lord". Of course, the reality of separation, the loneliness after 38 years of marriage, the finality and the endless, legal forms that had to be filled out were oppressive. But throughout those days, I was thankful that Dick was FREE, rejoicing with the whole company of heaven! My loss was a result of self-pity – but I knew beyond a shadow of a doubt that *Dick was totally healed in the Larger Life*!

When I had time, I re-read what I had written many years before in my second book, *HEALING ADVENTURE*, concerning "A Christian Attitude to Death" (pg. 28). My spirit bore witness to those words in a new way as now I had experienced the reality and could share this more effectively with others. God would ease my pain and use me in a new ministry to help others! It is very hard for those who have been bereaved to accept words of comfort from those who have not been through that shattering experience – but I could say: " I have wept where you weep and God has given me His Peace. He will give it to you if you will turn from self-pity over what might have been and give thanks for the years He gave you with your loved one who is now healed in the Presence of Jesus". A friend had sent me a little booklet that gave helpful advice. Whenever I found myself stressed by circumstances, I learned to say "For this I have Jesus". In time, I heard the still, small

Voice replying, "For this you have Me"! This was a tremendous comfort at that difficult time in my life!

Truly, my greatest comfort was in knowing that Dick was a born-again, Spirit-filled Christian – and that some day we would meet again! If any one reading this book has not surrendered your life to the Lord, please invite Jesus into your heart *now* to be your Lord and Master. You may feel that you have "lost control of your life" through a serious illness or a crippling accident – but NOW is the day of salvation, wholeness, healing of your relationships with Your Creator, with others and even with yourself – when you claim Jesus as your Savior! Don't wait until it is too late – begin *now* to rejoice in the Lord's taking control over your life as He gives you His Peace that passes understanding. For your own sake, and that of your loved ones, do it *now*! Write your own passport to eternity with Jesus!

In the months that followed, my ministry brought me great comfort although I had to make a serious decision: "Would I go on giving my life through VMTC to help save other people's marriages when my own had ended?" Again I prayed for the Lord's Highest Will to be done in my life – and the Wisdom and Strength were given to go on! The Lord reminded me of the meaningful Scripture that He had given me the day before he called Dick Home: "But you, be sober in all things, endure hardship, do the work of an evangelist, fulfill your ministry." *(II Timothy 4:5)* When our prayers are not answered in the way we would choose, we need to submit our wills to His Will – and wait on Jesus to show us how to let Him make us better, not bitter!

During the years that followed, doors began to open miraculously – so that in the past 23 years, I have been empowered to take VMTC ministry to many countries in Europe as well as to Australia, New Zealand, Malaysia, Indonesia, Singapore, the Philippines, Pakistan and Kenya. The prophecy that was given to me by the Lord (through one of our Directors and his wife) overwhelmed me on first hearing it: that I was to go into all the world and take the good news that Jesus came to give sight to the blind, open prison doors and set the captives free. *(Luke 4:18-19)* Our Board of Directors confirmed this prophecy. As more pastors were added to the Board, our VMTC training Schools for Clergy and their suitable lay people were set up in England, Sweden, Finland, Australia, Canada, Pakistan, Norway and New Zealand. When in 1980 I became International Board Coordinator, my responsibilities grew – and the Lord was always wonderfully faithful to provide the funds and leadership to help me spread this Scriptural, balanced, effective ministry: to transplant it abroad where it could bless others. The prophecy has now been fulfilled! To God be the Glory!

WINNING VICTORY IN SPIRITUAL WARFARE

CHAPTER VI

THE CALL TO AUSTRALIA

Speaking to 1500 people at the Australian National Charismatic Conference in 1975 in Melbourne was an exciting challenge! Others on the list of speakers were celebrities of charismatic renewal from many different countries: Canon Michael Harper of England, Bishop Ban It Chiu of Singapore, Revs. Loren Cunningham and Graham Pulkingham of USA and several other well known leaders. My daily workshops during the Conference were giving me the desired opportunity to share teaching about VMTC as they were attended by about 300 people. (Sadly, as a part of spiritual warfare, my books, which are my teaching tools, had failed to arrive in time!) Also, we were scheduled to lead a Weekend Teaching Mission and "Healing of the Whole Person" Retreats in several large cities of Australia after the 5-day Conference ended. On Friday morning, Alan Langstaff, the Director of Temple Trust, called me into his office and urged me to bring VMTC ministry to be transplanted in Australian soil! In order to expedite this move of the Spirit, he was inviting me to return to his country to speak at the two even larger Conferences the next year – one to be held in Brisbane and the other in Adelaide! This was a *tremendous* answer to our prayers for the Lord to open doors of ministry in the Land of the Southern Cross!

With the help of two of our US Board Members, my prayer partner and I returned the next winter – summer for them! As could be expected, there was some confusion in trying to set up Clergy Schools half-way around the world – but we earnestly prevailed in prayer against the enemy's attempts to disrupt the Schools. Many clergy and their wives who had attended my workshops in Melbourne came to these first two Schools – and some of them became the leaders when two years later, VMTC-Australia was set up as an incorporated ministry! Although Temple Trust had been our first covering of local authority, it became clear to Rev. Alan Langstaff and to us that the Holy Spirit needed a special venue suited to the needs of VMTC ministry. The Lord truly anointed their clergy and wives who made sacrificial commitments in order that VMTC could be rooted and grounded in Australian soil! The two major Conferences in 1976 were attended by capacity crowds and 1,000 people were turned away on the last night. The healings (spiritual, mental and physical as well as of relationships) in the seminars attended by 400 people made a real impact. Three weeks of ministry included speaking in Churches of many denominations in various cities, including two on the island of Tasmania where one service lasted till 2:00 AM because the needs were so great! It became obvious that I would have to take American Board Members (and my faithful prayer partner) twice a year so that the work would not lose momentum! Truly, the Holy Spirit empowered us all to work together in such unity and love that by August, 1978, the Schools were held in Sydney, Melbourne and Adelaide without the help of

American clergy as I was able to work entirely with their own leadership. Next, the Schools spread to Brisbane – and eventually across their continent to Perth! Part of the Lord's guidance was that we had Weekend "Healing of the Whole Person Retreats" for lay people along with the Clergy Schools in *each* city! Australian clergy and their wives were heroic in their consistent commitments to the heavy, sacrificial demands of spreading VMTC across their beautiful, large country! God's grace and provision has enabled me to keep my ministry under the authority of the Churches which have lovingly served interdenominationally – bringing healing to the Body of Christ.

Eventually, Australian leadership increased so that they have been holding 16 Clergy Schools a year – and have carried the heaviest part in the later years of transplanting VMTC to New Zealand. One of their past Presidents became very important in leading with me the transplanting of VMTC to Pakistan. This ministry has been heartily endorsed by Anglican and Uniting Churches as well as Pentecostal, Lutheran and charismatic independent Churches. Each of the 7 states in Australia has had VMTC Schools operating under the authority of their Board of Directors. My eighteen trips to Australia (some twice a year) were demanding in time, airfares and energy – but I have been blessed by many cherished relationships as the Holy Spirit has empowered us all to work together "to set the captives free, give sight to the blind and open prison doors". For those many years, Australia became my "second country". It was always a comfort to me to remember that my husband had approved of this long-range ministry before he went "Home to the Lord"!

It was during these years that I made so many trips around the world. Sometimes, circumstances would require that I fly to Sweden or Finland and lead a Weekend Retreat before beginning a Clergy School. Often I would take with me a lay woman prayer partner and one of our U.S. Directors to help lead the School. They would return to the States while I would fly on to Singapore where I was blessed to stay in a lovely Christian Hotel after leading a Weekend Retreat and a Teaching Mission in the Cathedral (or in one of their many renewed Anglican Churches). I would fly on to Australia where again I would lead a Weekend Retreat followed by a School. Often, I flew later to another city to begin the same process! The Holy Spirit opened these doors of opportunity to transplant VMTC ministry abroad – and He gave me the supernatural empowering to carry on such heavy ministry schedules. In retrospect, I'm overwhelmed – but at the time, the Lord's joyous anointing carried me through each heavy engagement! On one occasion, I was needed in Sabah with an Australian pastor to minister to the Bishop's wife. The enemy's attack was especially heavy and I lost my voice – but in spite of it, the Lord worked His miracles! As soon as our five-hour ministry had ended, my voice was totally restored! Satan had tried to thwart our ministry – but he failed! Praise God!

Weather conditions sometimes made it preferable to reverse the direction – so I would begin my round-the-world ministry trip by flying to Honolulu to spend the night – and then leave at midnight on the next night for Australia. The U.S. Team that went with me would return home after we finished our ministry in two or three Australian cities – and I would fly on to Singapore or Malaysia or Indonesia!

On one occasion, an Australian Director and his wife went with me to help lead ministry in Jakarta on our way to the International Board Meeting in Sweden. Sadly, that was the year that VMTC-Great Britain withdrew from VMTC's International Board. Only the Lord could have equipped me with the wisdom, the physical stamina and the Love for these many nationalities. Because Jesus carried me through these strenuous years (1974-1995) I never had to miss an engagement – it was truly His miracle! I still don't like to travel – but my commitment made so many years ago in 1947 when He healed my son of asthma has been fulfilled: "to help restore the healing ministry to the Church in any way He chose." Many years later, my first interpretation of tongues was: "Go ye into all the world and preach the Gospel in My Love – and fear not any man!" The Lord gives us a call – and if our hearts are obedient, He gives us the open doors and the spiritual, mental and physical equipping we need to walk through those doors! Praise God!

I thank God for the many Directors and lay women prayer partners who also responded in obedience and were important to the fulfilling of this call. One U.S. Board Member who originally made fun of the name Victorious Ministry Through Christ, later made three trips to Australia with me! How many times our teams have been reminded by the Lord of His words to those disciples who were double-minded about following Him: "No one who puts his hand to the plow and looks back is fit for the kingdom of God". *(Luke 9:62)* We thank God for the loving and selfless commitment of *each* of the hundreds of team members who have cheerfully (without remuneration) over the years helped to staff our VMTC Schools of Prayer

Ministry throughout the USA – as well as abroad! They are too numerous to mention but I am sure that their names are "written in heaven". We thank God for the dedicated leadership He has raised up in each country to accept VMTC training – to establish their own Clergy Schools of Prayer Ministry as they faithfully took up the torch we handed them: to extend and protect this ministry from misuse wherever the Lord has rooted and grounded it in His Love!

Through the trials of this far-flung ministry, I have come to know the marvelous provision of God and the extent of His Resources. Truly, as Paul wrote in his Epistle to the *Philippians*: "my God will supply every need of yours according to his riches in glory in Christ Jesus". *(4:19)* Through many trials, Paul learned: "in whatever state I am, to be content. I know how to be abased, and I know how to abound; in any and *all* circumstances I have learned the secret of facing plenty and hunger, abundance and want" (*vs 11-12*, italics mine). Could any of us write such words from an imprisonment that seemingly was crippling the missionary ministry of such a great evangelist and apostle? Or would our words be of self-pity – instead of joy in the Strength of the Lord? God has always been faithful to supply the Power when we supplied the willingness! He awaits the total commitment of our lives to Him!

In the later stages of transplanting the VMTC ministry to a foreign country, it was easier because I could use their local leaders to direct and staff their Schools. The Lord had laid it on Dick's and my hearts that I should never take a salary or any income from my books or speaking ministry –

even though I was working full-time, plus a great deal of overtime! This enabled VMTC to subsidize airfares and motel expenses for our traveling teams to so many far away places. The countries' National Boards paid for our local accommodations and gave VMTC-USA the offerings from my many speaking engagements to help with part of our heavy travel expenses. But VMTC-USA invested well over $150,000 to subsidize this vital overseas outreach! Many, many thankful people have contributed generously (and often very sacrificially) to make possible this extension of Jesus' ministry: "to set the captives free, give sight to the blind and open prison doors". *(Luke 4:18,19)* To God be the Glory!

Paul wrote to the Corinthians: "God loves a cheerful giver. And God is able to provide you with every blessing in abundance, so that you may always have enough of everything and may provide in abundance for every good work." *(II Corinthians 9:7-8)* Thanks to God's great goodness in providing for us financially through the generous obedience of so many people, we have been able to take VMTC Ministry to many countries. The Lord has met our needs! God's gifts vary. It is important *that we thankfully use the gifts He bestows upon us to His glory*! We are not to covet others' gifts, of course. We cannot out-give God – as those of us who tithe regularly have long been aware! He has His own "ways and means" committee and He will provide in the most unexpected ways – out of His bountiful Love – for our needs!

One winter, I was beginning a very expensive trip of ministry around the world when airfares for our team had suddenly increased, exceeding our expectations. The countries involved would barely be able to meet their respective quotas for my airplane ticket – and VMTC-USA was to pay for all of the team's fares! The Lord had given us clear assurance concerning our original plans prior to the increase in fares; and when a final check was made in prayer (before purchasing the last team member's ticket for $300.00), His assurance remained strong and clear: "Go in faith, nothing doubting!" From New York, I called our Treasurer just ten minutes before boarding time – much to his delight, as he had been wondering how to reach me to tell me of a most wonderful and unexpected gift check received that afternoon just after I left home! The Lord had, in answer to our prayers, guided and prompted a successful young farmer not to lay up treasure in enlarged barns but to sell that "windfall crop" and send a check for $2000.00 to Victorious Ministry Through Christ. What amazing timing – possible only because this young Christian layman and his wife were truly *obedient to the Lord's Voice of guidance*! He had been blessed by the Lord through receiving VMTC Prayer Ministry – and then had been trained in our Schools to help his pastor bring the same joyous release to others. What true thanksgiving was expressed in their desire to help underwrite such a large part of the cost of our first School in Singapore! Scripture gives a wise warning and a meaningful promise, not only to those who farm but to all of us: "...he who sows sparingly will also reap sparingly, and he who sows bountifully will also reap bountifully". *(II Corinthians 9:6)*

Some years after this, it became clearer that I was to sell my house and buy one in an excellent "retirement village" where I would have maintenance and security – a wise move in view of my extensive travels. However, it would mean that VMTC would no longer have free office space in my home – and that the cost of renting a suitable office suite would be added to our budget. Although I tried to solve the problem by selling my house at a higher price, my efforts were unsuccessful. One evening just before Christmas, a very committed business man (who had been greatly blessed by this ministry) called me to say that the Lord was guiding him to advise me to go ahead and sell my house, without being concerned over the cost of future office rental. He assured me that his corporation would provide the necessary funds! What a wonderful Christmas present! And to this day, he and his wife have most generously been the Lord's Provision for VMTC's needs – praise God!

"Now to him who by the power at work within us is able to do far more abundantly than all that we ask or think, to him be glory in the church and in Christ Jesus to *all* generations, for ever and ever. Amen." (*Ephesians 3:20-21)*

CHAPTER VII

OVERCOME BY THE SPIRIT

About midnight, we were napping on our flight from Honolulu to Manila where we were due to arrive very early Friday morning – in time to catch our flight for Baguio, a lovely, cool resort in the mountains. Suddenly the Captain came on the intercom to announce a change of flight plans. Our hearts sank as we heard the words: "We're requested as an emergency relief measure to divert our flight to Guam – so we will not arrive in Manila as planned! Our estimated time in Manila has been changed to 10:30AM. We are sorry for this inconvenience." Inconvenience? Our flight plans were shattered as we were to have connected with a local Philippine flight, leaving for Baguio at 8:30AM! Obviously, that flight would have already departed by the time we arrived in Manila after our "relief detour" to Guam! The airline flight attendant was not at all helpful! There was only one flight a day to Baguio – and our hosts would be there worriedly awaiting our arrival as they were not aware of this "good-will emergency detour". I was to begin leading at 6:00PM a Weekend Retreat for missionaries and local church leaders – and the Dean of the Anglican Cathedral in Manila would have already flown to the Retreat Center to make preparations for us. My prayer partner and I began to pray for the Holy Spirit to guide us as we needed

His divine wisdom – and strength to face this totally unexpected challenge!

The "emergency delivery" was made to Guam and our plane took off again for Manila. When we arrived (somewhat later than the estimated 10:30AM) we inquired about alternate flights – but there were none! Fortunately, I could speak "Puerto Rican Spanish" and finally I established the fact that a local bus was our only alternative! We did not know how *local* that bus would be! It was a glorified jitney – no facilities, no air conditioning and no refreshments! The humidity was high and we did not dare drink water (or any of the local beverages) being hawked at the frequent stops – along with some greasy, unappetizing looking food that smelled of strange odors. We had no local money – but finally we were able to get two small bottles of coke. Of course, we knew that ice was out of the question although the native ices looked tempting. We prayed earnestly that each local stop would be the last as we reached the suburbs – for the long trip to the mountains seemed to be interminable! Sadly, the crowded, hot bus rumbled on from one village to the next, frequently stopping to take on new passengers after lengthy delays when our fellow passengers got off to buy more "local goodies". We were thirsty and hot and hungry – but we knew that sampling local food or drinks was dangerous! We prayed for strength to endure the four hours of swerving around hairpin turns in what seemed to us a very rickety bus for such a long journey. We were too tired and uncomfortable to sleep (even though we had flown all night over the Pacific and had looked forward to the scheduled afternoon's rest at the Retreat Center)! The Lord's Grace enabled us to endure the interminable trip – until finally we pulled into the Baguio Bus Station at 4:30PM where our hosts were anxiously awaiting our arrival.

What a blessing to be able to shower and change from our sticky clothes! There was hardly time to unpack and take a quick nap before we dressed and pulled ourselves together to join the retreatants for dinner. Praying in the Spirit had sustained us during the long journey – and now at last these were refreshments that we could safely eat! Never had I blessed a meal more whole-heartedly – even though some dishes were quite strange to us!

Before long it was time to start our evening meeting and we fortified ourselves in prayer as we reached the assembly room. But there was no one there! Stunned, we asked the Dean and the Arch-Deacon (who were our Co-leaders) where the people were. "Oh, they won't come for another half hour. We're on Manila time!" Fortunately, we could use this unexpected delay to pray that the Lord would put the anointing on us and thus enable us to flow together in the Spirit. My prayer partner and I had not known that the two men were competitive – but that soon became evident! My heart sank and I knew that I would have to carry most of the load of teaching. Finally, the people sauntered in – some were vacationing missionaries from other countries and others were local leaders from the Philippine Episcopal Church. Their Bishop had invited me to come to lead this Retreat because he was a friend of Bishop Ban It Chiu of Singapore (whom the Lord had been using to open doors for me to speak in several Far Eastern countries). Bishop Chiu was an important leader in charismatic renewal and had been very supportive of my ministry from the time we met at that first Temple Trust Conference in Australia early in 1975.

At last, we opened with choruses and prayers led by our two sponsoring dignitaries. I could tell that few of my audience spoke English fluently – so I had to speak very slowly, using simple vocabulary that they would be able to understand. In desperation, I prayed for the Holy Spirit to take over – and praise God, He did! Suddenly I hadn't the slightest idea what I was going to say – but the Holy Spirit gave me words that flowed out effortlessly and seemed to be meeting their needs. As I watched their faces, I could see the response that the Lord was bringing about in their hearts. I was so tired that I hardly knew what I was saying until after I heard myself speaking the words! It was an amazing experience to realize that the Holy Spirit could speak *through* me as I surrendered myself totally for Him to use! God knew their needs – even if I didn't! I even sensed that He was giving these people supernatural understanding of truths that they might otherwise not have been able to comprehend. As I was mid-way through my message, I glanced at my weary prayer partner – only to see that she had fallen asleep! But the people were alert and eager to hear. I prayed that the Lord would use me to heal their relationships – especially between my two clergy sponsors. Once, I really felt such numbness in my feet (very swollen after the long, hot day) that I could hardly stand. Truly, *the Lord had to take over as I was so weary that I felt I was half asleep* – and yet He was delivering *through me* a message that was evidently changing their hearts! I realized that when I supplied the willingness, He would supply the Power. To God be the Glory!

The Holy Spirit fell on this group that weekend! When we started on Saturday morning (a half hour late as was their custom) I was amazed to see that the Church was entirely open – only partly walled with huge windows. Just as it was time for me to speak, a swarm of pigeons fluttered toward me into the Church! My first thought at this invasion was to duck and sit down in utter frustration. Then silently, I heard within me the still, small Voice of the Holy Spirit – and I found myself beginning my message with God's Love for us all – even the birds of the air! What could have disconcerted me was used by the Lord to slant my message in a practical way – and again the Holy Spirit took over – so that I found myself saying things that I had not planned to say. But the words were evidently the right ones! The people became most responsive – and I felt God's holy supernatural Peace come over us. During the mid-morning break, they provided us with tiny boiled sweet potatoes and coffee! God's Love was truly touching them that weekend in a new way! Their response was miraculous! The Lord had used my utter weariness to show me that when I was the most empty, He could use me by filling me with His Holy Spirit – empowering my spirit and mind and body to serve Him! I have learned over the years since then that rather than prepare a rigid outline for a message, it is more important for me *to empty myself and prayerfully prepare to listen to the Holy Spirit who will lead me to speak the Truth that will glorify Jesus*! The Holy Spirit knows the hearts of the listeners – so I need only to be open to His leading! I had to learn to *trust Him totally* – not my own intellect. I had to be prayerfully pliable in His anointing, my thoughts and will surrendered to HIS WILL! When the weekend ended, the Dean and the Arch-deacon were most gracious in their comments and the overwhelming Love of God had brought us all (including them) into a beautiful unity – truly an answer to our fervent prayers!

When we returned to Manila a year later, we had another sponsor in the American Bible Society. Once again, the Lord provided wonderful experiences of His life-changing Power! In one meeting, a young woman was brought to me for intensive prayer as she had never been able to speak. In the Spirit, I discerned that a demonic spirit was binding her, keeping her from being able to speak. She had heard the message that I had given about Jesus the Savior who heals and delivers and sets the captives free. The Lord's anointing came on me to bind and cast out that possessing spirit which had kept her dumb for so many years. She opened her eyes wide and out of her mouth came her first words: "Thank you, Jesus! I love you, Jesus!" She was set free by the Power of the Holy Spirit from that demonic possession – so that she could then receive Christ as her Savior and be baptized. Pagans can be possessed by the devil. We recall that in *Acts 10:38*, Luke writes of "Jesus of Nazareth, how God anointed Him with the Holy Spirit and with power and He went about doing good, and healing all who were oppressed by the devil; for God was with Him." And in *I Corinthians 12:3*, we read: "...no one can say 'Jesus is Lord', except by the Holy Spirit." Christians belong to Jesus – therefore as "born again" believers we cannot be possessed by evil powers. We are saved by Jesus when we accept Him as Lord and Master. Christians can however be *pressed* by the devil – *de*pressed, *op*pressed and even *ob*sessed – but not "*possessed*" because possession means ownership – and we are temples of the Holy Spirit! The danger of playing around with witchcraft and Satanic forces is that we can open ourselves to the controlling influence of demonic powers. Many Scriptures (both Old and New Testament) warn us of these dangers. We fail to heed God's Word at our own peril! We need the wisdom of the Lord and all the other gifts of the Spirit in our ministry "to set captives free"!

The Lord opened doors of ministry for me in several other Far Eastern countries through the kind recommendations of Bishop Ban It Chiu, whom you may recall I had met in January, 1975 when my prayer partner and I had flown to Melbourne, Australia to speak at the very large Temple Trust

Conference sponsored by Rev. Alan Langstaff. Alan and Dorothy had visited the USA several years prior to that event when I was speaking at Melodyland in California. I had brought a trained team with me as we were to do VMTC ministry in between my speaking sessions. When it was announced that people could sign up for appointments, about 70 names confronted us – more requests then we could possibly meet! Nevertheless, we felt that we were to minister to a young pastor from Australia who had unexpectedly arrived as a guest at our hostess' lovely home. When Alan was so greatly blessed by this ministry, he said to me: "I feel that I am speaking prophetically – and that some day I'll be inviting you to come to speak in my country." I replied that I felt so, too. I had great confidence in his prayers because I had seen him fasting at the table and praying for God to provide the funds for his wife to join him at Melodyland – a seeming impossibility! We were overjoyed with him when she walked in the door! The Lord had miraculously provided Dorothy's airfare in answer to Alan's believing prayers of faith!

As previously related, my ministry had already been set up in England and Sweden – so I was very busy and had forgotten about this incident. Just before Christmas in 1973, the prophesied letter of invitation arrived. Alan Langstaff had been used by God to shepherd charismatic renewal in Australia and he was now the founder of Temple Trust which was staging large charismatic conferences. Among the ten invited speakers were Revs. Michael Harper and Dennis Bennett (both of whom I knew) but also Bishop Ban It Chiu whom at that time I had not yet met. My husband and I prayed about the invitation – and he did not feel led to go with me. But he was in *total agreement* that I should accept this opportunity to take VMTC ministry to this far away continent! So, I wrote Alan my acceptance and asked that I could be accompanied by my long-time prayer partner. I was later very thankful that Dick had whole-heartedly given his blessing – because about a month afterwards (on January 27th) Dick was stricken with what proved to be his third heart attack – and he lingered in a coma for nineteen days before the Lord called him Home on February 15, 1974. It was agonizing for me to watch his life fading away!

Three months later, in May, it became absolutely necessary for me to go on with VMTC outreach in England and Finland in spite of my own heart-ache and personal loss after 38 years of marriage! I knew that this is what Dick would want me to do – and yet the extreme "loneliness of leadership" at such a time of loss made this the hardest "trial by fire" in my life. *(TRIAL BY FIRE, pp 5 -7)* Endless paper-work and practical decisions weighed heavily on me – but our wonderful neighbors (who loved Dick like a brother) volunteered their help. Lester became the Treasurer not only for VMTC but also helped me in so many practical ways and in keeping up with my personal finances. He had been closer to Dick than to his own brothers. Although Charlotte was not a secretary, she managed the correspondence and book orders as well as giving me loving support in practical ways too numerous to mention! They insisted that I must continue to live in our home, saying, "because if you move away, it will be harder for us to help you!" They cheerfully provided transportation to and from the airport when I traveled and took loving responsibility for Dick's mother when the ministry took me away from home. As Dick was an only child, I had inherited my mother-in-law on February 15, 1974 – and had full responsibility for her well-being and finances! Fortunately, God had made it possible for her to live in recent years in an excellent retirement home – so that I did not have physical care of her during the more than a year that she lived after Dick had "gone Home to the Lord". These dear, thoughtful neighbors gave her the loving attention she needed in my absence – and they insisted that I go on with my ministry, even though it was going to take me to many foreign countries as VMTC was expanding in Europe to Sweden and Finland. They felt that God had called them to be my "support team". Even though they had never received the ministry and did not fully understand charismatic renewal, they gave their time and practical help so that I could keep my home – with our guest suite of 3 rooms as VMTC's office.

How wonderfully the Lord provides in a time of our greatest need – in order to fulfill His Promises and Purposes for our lives! During the many years of frustration because of the Navy's continued moves, I had no awareness that God was training me to be His traveling missionary! I had long had a sense of destiny – that He had more in store for me – but I could not believe (until I found it happening) that God was really going to send me "into all the world to preach the Gospel in His Love – and fear not any man"! In the earlier years when I worked so hard for IBM, I had no inkling that God would indirectly use that experience in business planning to prepare me to know how to set up detailed scheduling and training Schools and Christian counseling in 8 other countries as well as 11 times a year across the U.S.A.! What a joyous empowerment it has been to know that I was moving in the center of the stream of *His* Highest Will for my life! When you and I supply the willingness to be obedient to His Will, our omnipotent Lord supplies the Power to enable us to carry out His Will! To God be the Glory!

WINNING VICTORY IN SPIRITUAL WARFARE

CHAPTER VIII

HE WILL GIVE HIS ANGELS CHARGE OVER YOU

We were speeding down the heavily trafficked highway in Malaysia, the country supposed to have the highest accident death rate for missionaries, when the three of us in the back seat of the black Mercedes began to pray in the Spirit with a sudden urgency. Then it happened! Our car crashed into the one ahead – and the impact made us spin off to the left, headed across the busy highway toward the ditch. As our prayer languages became more insistent, we looked up and suddenly our car safely veered away from the ditch on two wheels and was then headed in the opposite direction! A squadron of angels must have blocked it from turning over! As we began to praise the Lord, we opened our eyes – only to see another car speeding head-on toward us! Instinctively, we closed our eyes again and called on the Name of Jesus as a head-on collision was inevitable! When we opened our eyes again, the other car had vanished – and our Mercedes was swinging around across the road until suddenly it was headed in the opposite direction – just where we had been when the accident began! When our Malaysian driver was able to bring his car under control, he was very frightened, knowing that we could have suffered serious injuries. But none of us was really hurt. I had experienced a whip-lash in my neck but my co-leader, the Dean of the Anglican Cathedral in Singapore, was only shaken up a bit. My thoughtful prayer partner for this Weekend Retreat found some ice (when at last we arrived at the Conference Center) and she filled her shower cap to make a hastily improvised ice-bag. So, after two hours of rest, the Dean and I (with her faithful intercessions) began to lead a 3-day Retreat on the "Healing of the Whole Person" at Camp Dixon near Kuala Lumpur – in the joy of the Lord who had saved our lives from sudden destruction! However, we agreed it was wisdom to get a different driver to take us to the Airport when our time of ministry had effectively ended! (*Psalm 91:11*)

The Lord's Prayer tells us that we can pray "Deliver us from evil" – but so often we let fear control us when we most need to use our faith to call on the Lord and know that He hears us and that He can and will deliver us from evil! In *II Timothy 1:7*, we read: "God has not given us a spirit of timidity but of power and love and discipline." *His* is the power to overcome with good what Satan intends for evil – but He can work more miracles in our daily lives when we pray in faith instead of panicking! The perfect Love of Jesus casts out fear in a way beyond our limited human understanding when we call upon *His* Name. The sound mind referred to in this Scripture is also explained as "discipline" – not a mind that is so obsessed with fear and anxiety over life's troubling circumstances that it creates problems. "For what I fear comes upon me, and what I dread befalls me." *(Job 3:25)* Our fears can open the door of our minds so that the enemy can attack us with his lies and false accusations. Fear is negative expectancy. It is much like driving our car in reverse – instead of forward in the Power of the Lord! Fear can paralyze us so that we do not hear and act upon

God's guidance. How often Jesus spoke the words "Fear not" and He speaks them to us today.

"Faith comes by hearing and hearing by the Word of God" is a truth that no one can deny. Faith grows as we use it in the daily-ness of life – so that when the big problems arise, we will be able to see that *Jesus is the "Problem-Solver"* and we can release all our needs to Him! Faith is also a precious and much-needed gift of the Holy Spirit – one we can call upon the Lord to give us – when our human faith would be too weak. Faith is acting upon the promises of God – taking them to be true and believing for the answer *before* we see it. As *Hebrews 11:1* says: "Faith is the assurance of things hoped for, the conviction of things not seen." God uses our faith to create the answer – but often, we are giving Him only wishful thinking! Our unbelief can hold back His answer. Because He has created us with freedom of choice, we can trust in Him, or we can allow double-mindedness to rob us of the Victory we could be experiencing. Satan will often bombard us with fearful thoughts, so we need to put on each day the helmet of Salvation to protect our minds from these assaults. Praying in the Spirit is a wonderful blessing! Praising the Lord is an important antidote in times of spiritual warfare and it quickens our awareness of our need to rely on Jesus – *to let Him take charge of our lives*! Although Satan (as the deceiver) may set traps for us, we do not have to fall into them if we keep our eyes fixed on Jesus. When we become fearful or angry, we play into the devil's scheme to stir up rebellion against God's Purposes for our lives. Satan has often been called "the accuser" and also "the deceiver of the brethren". His "pincer movement" is to create opportunities for us to respond in fear, self-pity, anger, rejection, rebellion or lust – and then, when we do react in this way, he is quick to accuse us, putting burdens of guilt on us! If, on the contrary, we respond to life's pressures with trust in the Power of Jesus as the Overcomer, Satan becomes a defeated foe! What Jesus did at Calvary is *reality* – but if we do not know and exert our "throne rights" as Christians, Satan will try to bluff us out of the Victory that is ours to claim. In *Revelation 3:21-22* we read: " 'He who overcomes, I will grant to him to sit down with Me on My throne, as I also overcame and sat down with My Father on His throne. He who has an ear, let him hear what the Spirit says to the churches.' " Praise God that His divine Protection can be ours!

How can we overcome? Not in our own human strength but in acknowledging our frailty, our weakness, and calling upon the Power of the Lord. In *Luke 10:17*, He has given us power and authority to use His Name – but only if we commit ourselves to Him! *James 4:7* tells us: "Submit therefore to God. Resist the devil and he will flee from you." So, God's Word tells us that we are not to be passive Christians – but, on the other hand, we do not want to tangle with the enemy *unless we are submitted to the Lord*. We can wear the badge of authority because of what Jesus has *already* done for us at Calvary. "There is Power in the Blood" is more than a hymn. It's a reality that Jesus bought for us when He overcame the power of Satan at Calvary! Jesus was the only person good enough to pay this price – but because He did this out of total commitment to the Father's Will, you and I can go FREE when we exercise our faith in the Word made Flesh – Jesus the Christ, the Son of God, the Anointed One! We like to claim God's Promises, but too often we want to overlook the conditions that are attached to them. The devil will not flee from us unless we are willing to be committed to the Lord and stand against his wiles, deceits and temptations in the Power of Jesus Christ! We are doomed to defeat if we try to resist in human power alone.

When we give over the reins to the enemy in life's confrontations, we hold back the Kingdom of God which we are all called as Christians to help establish on earth. Satan is a robber and a thief – and he would like to cheat us out of our rightful position in Christ. We always have the deciding vote: Jesus voted for us and Satan voted against us – but *we* choose which voice we will listen to! Will we listen to the Voice of the Shepherd or that of the robber? WE have to use our God-given freedom of will in a way that glorifies Jesus – or we may be slipping into the enemy's snares. Praising God in the midst of crises or turmoil is not always easy as we have to crucify the flesh (our natural instincts) to do this. But, it is a sure antidote to self-pity; and it dissipates fear and dissolves anger. We choose many times a day whether we will go Jesus' Way of love, trust and forgiveness – or whether we will give in to the nagging voice of the enemy who is our persistent adversary in spiritual warfare. Satan wants to deceive even the elect – those of us who have elected to follow Jesus! We have the same enemy that Jesus had! But, we also have the same Heavenly Father who equips us to withstand Satan's attacks as He overcomes evil with good! Praise God!

When the Israelites went into battle, the praisers went before them. If we praise God with our first thought each morning, we can begin the day in His Presence and thus be better prepared for whatever is to come. *Psalm 100* tells us to "enter into His gates with thanksgiving, and His courts with praise". Jerusalem, like many other cities, was a walled city and people entered in each day through its gates. God inhabits the praises of His people – so as we enter by the Gate of Thanksgiving, we can move on into the Courts of Praise. Praise helps us to establish our priorities for the day and so discover the Lord's Purposes. Then we can receive *His Power to fulfill His Purposes*! Someone once said: "If you don't meet the enemy coming toward you, you may be going his way!" Surely, we Christians need to heed Paul's warning to fight the good fight – against the deceits, discouragement, doubts, depressions and even despair that the devil tries to use to entrap or derail us in his rebellions against God's Purposes and Priorities. When we equip ourselves each morning with the whole armor of God, we do it out of our obedience to the Word where Paul warns his readers that they need this daily equipment. *(Ephesians 6:10-18)* We are putting on Jesus as we place each piece of armor to be ready for the day's battles. Jesus is our Commander-in-Chief and we are enlisted as His followers when we elect – commit ourselves – to follow Him. We will have the same enemy Jesus had – but we already know the end of the Book: JESUS WINS! Scripture warns us that Satan fell from Heaven where he had been an archangel named Lucifer – because of the rebellion and pride in his heart – and because of his violence. *(Ezekiel 28:15-17)* Is it any wonder that Satan stirs up violence today? We have taken prayer out of our schools and sadly it has been replaced with guns and drugs. God is calling us to become an army of "prayer warriors" to pray down the blessings of heaven on our land. In the "Prayer Vigils" at our VMTC Clergy Schools of Prayer Ministry we see how the Lord uses united, intensive, specific, anointed prayer to hasten His victories in people's lives. In his thriving Church in Times Square in New York City, Pastor David Wilkerson credits the effectiveness of their work to the powerful intercession which undergirds all of their ministry with the drug addicts and alcoholics, the homeless and abandoned families. Even secular sources are admitting that the crime rate has dropped noticeably in that area. Their "half-way" houses do an effective ministry because they are undergirded and financially supported by intensive, effective prayer. Should our Churches today be houses of believing prayer where miracles are expected and miracles take place? Scripture warns us that Satan is deceiving even the elect – so we can expect him to try to deceive us into thinking that we are too busy to pray! James, the half-brother of Jesus, wrote in the Epistle that bears his name: "The effective prayer of a righteous man can accomplish much". (*Vs. 5:16*) Do we pray enough for our President, the Congress and the Supreme Court to be guided back to the Christian principles upon which our country was founded? Isn't it part of Satan's wicked plan to set up his kingdom in rebellion against God's Purposes for the world? Is God calling each of us to be a "prayer warrior" – in our home and city – for the Lord to use us to overcome evil with good?

Intercessory prayer has been called "Love on its knees". Jesus has entered the Holy of Holies in Heaven and He is always interceding for us. (*Hebrews 7:25*) So we are never alone when we are praying in His Name (in agreement with His Nature). According to *John 14:13-14*, Jesus promises to do whatever we ask in His Name so that it will bring glory to the Father. But this means that our prayers need to be made with the mind of Jesus and for *His Purposes*! Obviously it means *that we are to know Jesus so intimately that we can pray His words* – not trying to change God's Will but rather to yield our prayers *totally to His Will*! We are to have such a close, abiding relationship with Him – formed out of constant obedience – so that we will know what pleases Him. The secret is given to us in *John 14:21*, "He who has My commandments and keeps them, he it is who loves Me; and he who loves Me shall be loved by My Father, and I will love him, and will disclose Myself to him". As we join our hearts and minds and wills with *His* Will, we will be able to ask in His Name and see our prayers answered as we serve Him in our ministry of intercession. Praising Him in song (whether in our own language or in an unknown tongue) builds faith. Giving to others is an expression of God's Love through us as well as of obedience to His call to share cheerfully of what He has entrusted to us. It is a practical way of showing forth our praise!

The prayer of faith is the greatest gift we can give to someone who is caught in the "trials by fire" of spiritual warfare – when spirits of helplessness and hopelessness are the mental attacks that Satan wages against them. The prayer of faith accepts the fact that our prayer is already being answered – so we thank God in advance. Faith is thanking God *before* the answer comes. Even when we do not immediately see the results of our prayers, we need to hold that person before the Throne of Grace in thanksgiving. Our intercessory prayers can shield that person from the enemy's attacks if we do not doubt in our hearts – if we claim the answer and not the problem! It is, of course, most helpful if the one for whom we are interceding will join with us in a prayer of real thanksgiving, believing that he is receiving the needed blessing which will glorify God. It is helpful for us to *live* in an attitude of prayer. What would Jesus say or do in this situation that confronts us? What does the Word of God tell us to think or say or do? Aligning our wills with His Perfect Will is not always easy to do. Sometimes we need to pray: "Lord, make my present relationship with this person what *You want* it to be!" Praying in the Spirit (as the Holy Spirit prays through us) is particularly helpful when we really do not know how to pray. Persevering in prayer is difficult in many cases – but both Jesus and Paul gave us lessons on this important need. "Stick-to-it-tivity" is a characteristic God will honor because it means being steadfastly obedient to His call on us to pray without ceasing. We cannot always be on our knees literally, but our hearts and minds can be committed to praying for His Highest Will to be done! To God be the Glory!

CHAPTER IX

SALMONELLA IN PAKISTAN

Traveling to different countries can present health hazards, not just inconveniences and frustrations. Long sleepless nights in crowded seats on drafty planes can be very wearying – especially if one misses an important connecting flight and arrives at the destination hours later than expected! Lost luggage can be a horrible reality – so one has to plan carefully and then struggle with heavy "carry-ons" – in case the checked luggage goes to the wrong destination. The undergirding of earnest intercessory prayer by fellow-Christians at home can make a vast difference. I used to mail out my detailed itinerary not only to those sponsoring my speaking engagements abroad but also to a list of "prayer warriors" whom I could trust to pray many times a day – *not* just "when they felt like it"! Real intercession is not just a casual prayer when one feels like it: it is "praying through" each event against interference by the enemy who would like to thwart God's Purposes, often in different and unexpected ways. Scriptures in many, many places remind us that it is the "prayer of faith" – believing *before* we see the answer, thanking God in advance – that really counts! God removes mountains of doubt and fear, of unforgiveness and bitterness, of self-pity and self-condemnation in response to our prayers of faith. He heals the sick and forgives our sins when we accept His Promises by faith and act upon them. Before we see the answer, we can have the conviction that it will come to pass – we are told in *Hebrews 11:1.* "Believe that you have received them and they shall be granted you" is the real meaning of *Mark 11:24.* Most of us know this but we find it hard to practice such faith! David Wilkerson says "Your only way to a full and complete victory is to *FAITH* your way out of your crisis"!

Why is it so hard for us to have faith in some situations and not in others? Often it is because *we* have the pain or the problems! It is always far easier to have faith for others. We need that sense of "immediate connection with God" when we can hear His still, small Voice in spite of the clamor of our busy, pressured lives. God does not send illness to get our attention – but He can use it! Satan uses infirmity to try to defeat us – and sometimes we feel almost overwhelmed and stressed out by these attacks, both large and small. *We need each other* as we try "to win the race and fight the good fight" against evil that so often seems to be constant and overwhelming in today's spiritual warfare. It helps to read Peter's Epistles or Paul's encounters in the *Acts of the Apostles* (also called the *Acts of the Holy Spirit*) – especially if we are battling doubt or self-pity or hopelessness. We have not yet been stoned or jailed because of our faith! God promised the Israelites that He would do battle with their enemies because they were in a Covenant relationship with Him. When the Assyrians came against them, the Angel of the Lord killed 185,000 in one night – all because they had humbled themselves before God and put their sole trust in Him! *(Isaiah 37:33)*

On one of my many trips to Pakistan, the spiritual warfare proved to be particularly difficult. Tense political conditions often seemed to be stirred up just before we arrived so that a curfew was threatened. On one occasion when I had left home a night early, so as to have an extra day to rest in Frankfurt, Germany, the passport visa regulation was suddenly changed – so that I was barred entry to my plane because I had not known in time to get that *important* document before leaving home! In *FREED TO LIVE*, you can read the detailed story of how the Lord intervened for me and miraculously enabled me to enter Karachi without a visa – in spite of being refused initially the right to board my plane (pp 40-42). God's provision for us is limitless. We are the ones who set limits because of our lack of faith!

On another occasion, two of our Team Members from Finland arrived a day late for our very tightly scheduled Clergy School of Prayer Ministry in Karachi because of intense spiritual warfare concerning their visas. God answered all of our earnest prayers for them and for the volatile, local, political situation with a miracle – and the blessings received by all at that School rewarded us for the extra commitment of time and energy to "pray through to victory" – unceasing prayers of faith – on their behalf. Sometimes spiritual warfare takes the form of division amongst the Team Members – and it takes the Lord's reconciling Love and Power to overcome what Satan intends for evil. The Scripture has so often proved true: "the things impossible with men are possible with God". *(Luke 18:27)* Perseverance in prayer is a *must* – whether we feel like it or not! God allows things to happen to test our faith which grows stronger when we use it as we keep our eyes on Jesus – even when it seems to us that the enemy is winning! The Victory may be just around the corner – but if we give up, we will lose our part in it.

During one of our most difficult ministry trips to Karachi, the plane on which we had been flying arrived twelve hours late at 4:00AM. I was *very* weary! A new person (whom I found to be deeply involved in psychic power) had been admitted to the School and I was greatly concerned about her suitability. My discernment proved to be true; and after two days, it became obvious to the other leaders (as well as to me) that she would need to be released from the School because of her unteachable attitude and unwillingness to accept the discipline and principles of the ministry. She had verbally attacked me from the very beginning; and though I forgave her, I could not condone the sin which was disruptive, affecting the well-being of others. In the midst of this spiritual warfare, I was suddenly stricken with salmonella! The medication I had brought with me soon ran out and the doses prescribed by the local hospital were horrible to taste and proved to be totally ineffective. Apparently, I had eaten some "fried rice" which the cook had made by using up scraps from the early morning's scrambled eggs – which after sitting out all day were contaminated and had caused my problem. It was frustrating enough to have to miss some of my teaching sessions – but the situation became alarming as days went on and I was still deathly sick with no sign of being able to travel – and no way to delay my departure flight! Although I had been anointed with oil and the local group had prayed for me, it was not until after the woman with psychic powers left the Monastery of the Angels that I began to feel better. Evidently, she had put a curse on me which we had not at first realized. But still, I felt so sick that I cried out, "Lord if I'm going to die, please don't let me die in Pakistan – get me *home*"! I counted the hours again and knew that there was no way I could travel (as sick as I was) in 24 hours! Suddenly, the still, small Voice told me to *pray for everyone* who had ever promised to pray for me – that "they would be jerked up to pray", no matter where they were! As the many names ran through my mind, I prayed for Jesus to call them to prayer – to alert them to my need. It was as if I were being led to wait while an orchestra was tuning up to play. Then unexpectedly, the Lord told me that my intercessors were ready and I was to pull myself out of bed and make a superhuman effort. In a voice of authority, calling on the Victory of Calvary and the Name of Jesus, I was to command Satan to leave me alone and rebuke the spirit of infirmity that had been attacking me with this illness! Once I did this, I was told clearly to begin to thank and praise God for the release from this vicious attack. And, as I did, I suddenly experienced *His Peace throughout my bodily organs, as well as in my heart and mind*! The symptoms disappeared and Jesus released His Strength in me – so that 24 hours later I was able, at the appointed time to board my plane for the long 2 day journey home with the usual necessary change of planes in Frankfurt! Thanks be to God who gave me the Victory! Needless to say, I prayed in thanksgiving for the "symphony of intercessors" whom the Holy Spirit had summoned in prayer to be a part of God's healing release of my body from the disabling throes of salmonella in Pakistan! To God be the Glory!

Because God desires for us to live in a love relationship with Him as His sons and daughters, He created us with freedom of will! We can choose to have an intimate relationship with Him or we can choose to live "I can do it alone" lives – depending only on our own resources. He wants us to spend "quality time" with Him each day so that when the crises come, we will be prepared. As Christians, we are to be believers who have sprinkled the Blood of Jesus on the doorposts of our hearts and minds – just as the Israelites claimed the protective power of the blood that they sprinkled on the doorposts of their homes on the night of Passover. We, today, need to trust in the power of God to deliver us from the enemy's vicious attacks in spiritual warfare. Our promised salvation through Jesus' Blood is not only for eternity to spend with Him – but also for the peace that comes in our daily living when we entrust our battles to Him! All victory comes from Him – not from our human power. Only He has the power to deliver us! In *Isaiah 54:17*, God promises us : "No weapon that is formed against you shall prosper, and every tongue that shall rise against you in judgment, you shall show to be in the wrong". What a comfort the Word of God is to us when we read, mark and inwardly digest it. We have to *appropriate God's Promises*, high-lighting them in our hearts, through the Power of the Holy Spirit. He will bring them to our recall in our time of need!

As one pastor recently said in an anointed sermon, "The world says: 'Make all you can so you can buy all you want.' But the Peace of God is *not* something that money can buy." In Hebrew, the real meaning of "prospering" is "having heart peace with God". Satan tempted Jesus in the wilderness and he will try to tempt us today to worship the many false gods – but our *real* security is in the Lord! Jesus responded with Scripture to each of the devil's three temptations. We, too, can resist the devil if we are submitted to Jesus. He is the One who gives us healing, deliverance, wholeness – as we put our *full* trust in Him! We can call upon Jesus' Name and stand on the power and authority of His Victory at Calvary as we wield the sword of the Spirit, the Word of God, so that we can be overcomers to glorify Him!

To pray in the Name of Jesus is to pray in His Nature – and that means death to the self-life. Each of us has a different cross and we can only bear it because of the Victory that Jesus has already won for us on the Cross. We have to yield ourselves so totally to Him that we can go through the cross to the Victory side – in spite of Satan's temptations to self-pity or self-aggrandizement or escapism. There will be new wounds and scars in the battle against the sins of the world and the deceits of the enemy. Our "purple heart" combat medal may be the willingness to forgive those who have rejected or scorned or betrayed us – especially those who have tried to manipulate us away from the call to obedience that Jesus has put in our hearts! He never called us to be successful but to be faithful! In His disciplining of us, we come to surrender ourselves, our hopes, our loved ones, our gifts, our very lives to Him who gave up His Life for each one of us – so that we can be changed more and more to His divine likeness. This refining is often a slow, ongoing process – and we at times cry out against the pain of dying to self. As the martyred prisoner, Dietrich Bonhoffer, wrote in *THE COST OF DISCIPLESHIP:* "When Christ calls a person, He bids them come and die" (to the self-life). God used him in solitary confinement (when most of us would have been crying over the Nazi prison camp's humiliation and starvation and torture) to leave this book as a legacy on the value of Christian suffering. It is so hard for us to accept the Scriptural challenge of "counting it all joy" when we are being tested for our willingness to follow Jesus at all costs – to put to death the self that wants to be esteemed and admired, and to bear other people's burdens – forgiving them when they sin against us. "Forgiveness is the Christ-like suffering which is the Christian's duty and privilege to bear" wrote Dr. Laurel T. Hughes in her excellent book, *COMBAT MANUAL* (p. 115). It is not easy – but unless we forgive others for their sins against us (or against those we love) we cannot really share in Jesus' redemptive work of the Cross. We can only do this by God's Grace – but unless we forgive others, we ourselves cannot be forgiven by God! Hanging on the Cross that first Good Friday, Jesus was battered and bloody, suffering excruciating pain – yet He prayed: "Father, forgive them; for they do not know what they are doing." *(Luke 23:34)* Can you and I do less than that as we walk today in the Master's foot-steps?

Forgiving others does not mean that we condone their sin. Sin is sin. But, when we forgive truly, we release that person and ourselves from a bondage, stronghold relationship. Although Satan may try to entrap us again by bringing back thoughts of old wounds, we need to stand on the promises of God – not our feelings! *(I Peter 2:1-5)* We have made a very important decision for Christ when we cancel the debt against someone who has hurt or abused or berated or deprived or belittled or betrayed us! (Ephesians 4:31-32) We can then plead the Blood of Jesus over the area of sin, submitting ourselves afresh to God, resisting Satan because we know that he has to flee. (James 4:7)

When we are standing on the Victory of Calvary as we are claiming our "Throne Rights" with Jesus, Satan no longer has a legal right to accuse us. *(Revelation 3:21)* To God be the Glory!

CHAPTER X

THE MINISTRY DEFINED

VMTC ministry involves Christians of various backgrounds. It is built on the foundation of Scripture, prayer, confession of sin, assurance of pardon (or absolution), forgiveness, freedom from bondage, deliverance and healing of wounds and scars of the past. This ministry is effective only for Christians because it builds on the firm foundation of Scripture – and unbelievers could not accept this presupposition. The wholeness we seek to minister is found in and through Scripture, which provides the sound basis so that Christians (from Assembly of God to Roman Catholics, Episcopalians, Lutherans, Presbyterians, Methodists, Baptists and those from other denominations, as well as non-denominational Christians) can minister together with amazing unity in the Love of Jesus the Healer. The empowering of the Holy Spirit enables those who minister in His name to use the Word of God to set the captive free! (*Luke 4:18, 19,21* and *Isaiah 61:1-4*)

As I wrote in *HEALING ADVENTURE*, my healing experience made me seek to know more of His will; to practice more of the principles of prayer which our Lord taught in His earthly ministry; to follow Him! *(Pg. 14)* This revolutionized my attitude toward God, toward my family and those about me. As a laywoman, I have sought to be used to bring His healing Love and Power into the lives of those whom He has brought into my life – not because I am worthy, but because He is worthy! I have seen His Love heal those bruised by the sin of the world; those filled with hate (as I once was); those victims of their own self-pity – the bitter, the fearful, the angry!

As has been pointed out in previous chapters, this healing adventure which was begun forty years ago, has involved me in the ministry of intercessory prayer in many different countries as far away as Japan, England, Scandinavia, Australia, Kenya, Pakistan and the Holy Land, as well as in many parts of America. Always our blessed Lord has revealed His healing Love. He is no respecter of persons, only conditions. The searching of Scriptures has convinced me that in healing the sick, our Lord was proclaiming the Will of God; that it is a human 'No' rather more often than God's 'No'. To be divinely healed means to surrender to Him! For many, this price is too great, too costly. For many, it is too hard to break free from the coddling of illness and once more assume full responsibility for life. For many, it is easier to take a pill than to give up a life-long habit, a grudge, a resentment or an overwhelming fear. But, after having witnessed the miracles of the healing Love of Christ in my own life and those with whom our Lord has led me to pray, I am sure that when we as the Body of Christ, the Church, provide a real climate of faith, His touch will have its ancient power! (*Acts 10:38*)

Twenty-five hundred years ago Hippocrates so wisely suggested treating the whole man. Later Plato said that one ought not to neglect the healing of the soul when making the effort to cure the body. We can be thankful for doctors both in England and America who have many centuries later confirmed the interaction between spirit, mind and soul – the relationships exemplified by our Lord in His earthly ministry of healing. We can be especially grateful for those doctors who pray with their patients – or meet regularly with pastors – to share the healing work of ministering to the whole man. It is wise to note the important part played by human emotions on the body.

The importance of forgiveness cannot be overemphasized! A crucial element in the act of confession of sin is the need to forgive. We are told in the Lord's Prayer: "Forgive us our trespasses, as we forgive those who trespass against us". *(Luke 11:4)* Again, when Peter came to Jesus asking Him: "Lord, how often shall my brother sin against me, and I forgive him? As many as seven times?" Jesus replied, "I do not say to you seven times, but seventy times seven." *(Matthew 18:21)* Scripture makes it clear to us that if we do not forgive others for their sins against us, God will not forgive us for our sins. *(Mark 11:25)* VMTC Prayer Ministry shows us that it is not as important what someone does to you or me as how we react to the situation. As an act of my will, I can forgive someone – not only that person who openly asks for my forgiveness, but also the one who may be completely oblivious to the need (or unwilling) to seek my forgiveness. I can be set free – but I need to forgive that person and seek forgiveness as an act of my will. God will give me the Grace to feel like it – *after I forgive*! When people say that they *can't* forgive, it is usually a situation where they *won't* forgive. The more mature we are, the more we are called to be the first to forgive! It may not be easy, but it is obedience to

God's Word.

Many people live in bondage to persons, places, things or past experiences as I was in my relationship with my mother-in-law. Only Jesus Christ can set us free from such bondages that are barriers to healing. As Paul wrote to the Galatians: "For freedom Christ has set us free; stand fast therefore, and do not submit again to a yoke of slavery". *(Galatians 5:1)* We rejoice that, as an important part of VMTC Prayer Ministry, we can be set free even from long-time bondages to persons, places, things or experiences – and not return to a yoke of slavery! Praise God that His Word is true! Our weapons are divinely powerful! *(II Corinthians 10:3-6)*

This ministry takes seriously Jesus' power, when necessary, to deliver people from spirits – whether they be of rejection, fear, anxiety, lust, anger, hopelessness, etc. – that may be oppressing a person. This can only be done in the power of the Holy Spirit, as we pray for the needed gift of discerning of spirits, one of the gifts listed in *I Corinthians 12*. Jesus gave power and authority to His apostles over unclean spirits. "And he called to him the twelve, and began to send them out two by two, and gave them authority over the unclean spirits." *(Mark 6:7)* We are His modern disciples and He equips us today to carry on His ministry through the gifts of the Holy Spirit. We are ineffective without them. Too often we try to do His work in our own strength or love. We need the supernatural empowering of the Holy Spirit to be effective. Deliverance is needed where an area in a person's life is *not* under the control of the Holy Spirit – but rather of a contrary spirit!

A thanksgiving prayer for healing by Jesus is always a

vital part of VMTC Prayer Ministry. Many people want to get well but not necessarily to be made whole! To be made whole means to have one's life so changed and freed from the past's brokenness that a fresh commitment can be made to Jesus the Healer. This final step of commitment in VMTC ministry makes wholeness a reality. Total Commitment means a total surrender to Jesus who alone can give the power to be healed and made whole – in spite of the deep wounds and fragmentations and sins of the past in a person's life. In effect, Jesus says to us today, as He did to the woman caught in adultery: "Go and sin no more". *(John 8:11)* He uses our faith today for those who may not in themselves have enough faith to believe Him for the miracle of a changed life. VMTC Prayer Ministry is biblical, Jesus centered and Spirit filled. The two (or three) mature ministers are trained to discern through gifts of the Holy Spirit and balanced teaching how to use a disciplined pattern to help people – under the authority of the Church. To God be the Glory!

While at a Clergy School of Prayer Ministry, I was given this prophecy from the Lord as a preface to a talk I was about to give on "Total Commitment". Hear what the Spirit is saying to the leaders of the Church today: "Repent and come apart from your sins of the spirit and of the flesh – and from the humanism which infiltrates and tarnishes your ministry. Set your heart and your priorities on Me, so that I may strengthen you to turn away from these sins and stand against the deceits and temptations of the world, the flesh and the devil. Pray in My Spirit for a new call to holiness so that the money-changers can be cast out and My people will be taught to respond to My call to total commitment, to depend on Me and seek to know My Voice amid the clamor of false prophets. There are so many false prophets today who are trying to call you away from obedience!

"When my Church becomes purified to be truly My Bride, I will return and call her to Myself. Glorify Me, your Lord and Master for that is who I am – not your 'cosmic bell-hop'. I love you: you are my Body, but your sins have made a separation between you and Me. Turn away from your idolatries and double-mindedness, from your rebellions against Me and My priorities on your lives. Repent and turn away from these wicked ways. Turn and live in the power of My Spirit. The abundant life does not consist of things. In My presence, you will know the abundance of My Love." To God be the Glory!

CHAPTER XI

SATAN IS A ROBBER AND A THIEF

To maintain the necessarily high standards for a Scriptural, balanced, disciplined ministry (such as VMTC is called to be) has been *very* costly! Over and over again, Satan has tried to deceive some of our leaders into thinking it was safe to ignore certain Scriptural principles and introduce others that were extraneous. Always there has been the temptation to make VMTC into a "quick fix" – instead of the thorough, Scriptural, balanced, accountable ministry where the basic team of two trained people (a man and a woman) listen and pray through the needs in a person's whole life, bringing that one to a deeper commitment to Jesus through the very real empowering of the gifts of the Holy Spirit! In some cases, people have argued over the need to have a trained man and woman team – but each of us has to have a mother and a father to get into this world! So, obviously we have male and female relationships that greatly affect us. The two team members have to be in agreement as they pray Scriptural prayers over all relationships discussed during the long session. This is not only a Scriptural procedure (because Jesus sent the seventy out two by two) but it is a safeguard against possible bias on the part of either team member. Also, the gifts are doubled! The Lord always chooses the right team if we pray and follow the guidance of the Holy Spirit. It is His ministry <u>through</u> them to the one in need. *(I Corinthians 12:8-11)*

In many cases, people have tried to introduce psychological techniques and psychic powers – in spite of serious warnings against these unwise additions. Our Board of Directors had to take a strong stand against serious changes made by the VMTC Trust which was set up in Great Britain many years ago – and of which I was originally a member. Sadly, a resolution of serious differences could not be effected, so I had to withdraw from their work. Necessarily, they changed the name of their ministry and gave up the right to carry on as VMTC-Great Britain. To our great sorrow, this affected the work which I had also set up in Sweden with their leadership help as well as that of several members of the U.S. Board of Directors. Sweden then withdrew (following Great Britain's decision) from the VMTC International Board! Fortunately, many years later, joyous reconciliation was effected with the Swedish Board through the help of two other countries who pointed out misunderstandings as being the devious work of Satan when he tried to destroy the unity of the growing VMTC Family! Swedish leaders then came to U.S. Schools and eagerly altered their work to conform to U.S. standards which had become International Board standards.

Years later, VMTC-Sweden, along with VMTC-Finland and VMTC-Pakistan, carried great responsibility for the spread of the work to Norway where eventually a National Board was set up and welcomed to the International Board. A similar problem (on a much smaller scale) was encountered in Pakistan when with the help of the U.S. and

Australian Boards (and some help from VMTC-Finland) I introduced the ministry there – after I had held a Weekend "Healing of the Whole Person Retreat" and a Teaching Mission in the Cathedral in Karachi. The Lord guided the Bishop to nip that division in the bud by declaring that there would be "only *one* VMTC ministry in Pakistan"! He had not only seen the results in bringing *real* renewal to his Diocese but also the lasting, life-changing effect that VMTC brought about in converts from Islam. A program using VMTC Prayer Ministry had enormously increased the effectiveness of their work with heroin addicts. The rate of success jumped to 80% when those who had come off the drug received VMTC ministry as it enabled them to deal effectively with root causes instead of only symptoms. Heroin addiction is one of their major social problems. Jesus sets the captives free when they want to be free!

VMTC-Canada had been established some years before that – after I had led a "Healing of the Whole Person Retreat" there. It was attended by several eager clergy couples who became key leaders. Of all the transplant operations, Canada was by far the easiest as our U.S. teams had only to cross the Ambassador Bridge from Detroit to Windsor! Their work had been accepted by the International Board – so, on one trip of ministry in Pakistan, a Canadian Director, also participated. At a more recent date, the Canadian Board attempted to work with the English "Wholeness Through Christ" when the latter tried to export their version of the ministry to Canada – but sadly, the work in England had been altered so seriously that reconciliation with them was impossible!

The enemy was still busily at work trying to divide and weaken this vital International work of the Spirit. Cracks began to appear in the unity. Unfortunately, some leadership failures gave Satan his chance. Because, as Founder, I had been VMTC World Coordinator for 12 years, it seemed right to our Board that leadership should become more inclusive of the other countries. It was decided that the Bishop should become President of "The Executive" of VMTC's International Board. Each of the four major countries would be represented by an officer on "The Executive": U. S. Board's Delegate would be the Secretary; Australia's would be the Treasurer; and Sweden's would be the Vice-President. Sadly, very serious misunderstandings arose when the VMTC International Board met in Sweden in 1994. Tensions mounted during the Meeting when some countries wanted to make serious changes in the wisely established VMTC patterns and procedures. This our Board could not accept! As the founding country, we had a special responsibility to God.

As a result of what the U.S. Board considered unauthorized delegation of authority to members of "The Executive", seemingly insurmountable problems arose! When the other countries objected strenuously to the resignation of our Delegate as Secretary, we felt rightly that they were interfering in the U.S. Board's national affairs. Angry Faxes did not help matters and only created more problems. It seemed to the U.S. Board that a terrible power struggle had developed which was not in keeping with the signed "Covenant Agreement" and "Standards Set as Goals" that had previously been solemnly and prayerfully accepted by all countries! At both the 1996 and 1997 U.S. Board Meetings, we agreed unanimously to notify once more "The Executive" (and all the other member countries) that they had broken the Covenant made with us and therefore they were to return to the U.S. Board the Director's Resource Files which had originally been given to them in trust under copyright provisions by the U.S. Board as the Founding Country. This meant that we were the only surviving country on the VMTC International Board! We had prayed and prayed for three years for *real reconciliation* – but sadly, no results could be seen. The way of repentance was being rejected by them – and without repentance there could be no real reconciliation.

Miraculously, in August, 1997, I received a most beautiful, contritely humble letter from "The Executive" which had just completed its Meeting in Norway. The tone of the letter showed the change of repentance from unjust maligning to a welcome attitude of loving respect – and I was being begged with all sincerity to attend their next Executive Meeting in September, 1998! It brought tears of joy to my eyes to read of their real change of heart and their request for forgiveness and reconciliation with me as Founder and Resource Person for VMTC International! I was able at once to forgive all the false accusations of the past and rejoice in their new attitude. Personal letters of similar nature have come from the leaders of all of the countries. Serious, remedial work lies ahead – but at least there is a new beginning in Christian Love.

Our Board has been notified of this wonderful news! Truly, only the Lord Himself could have brought about this miraculous change of heart and mind! I look forward to joining with these brothers-and-sisters-in-Christ as we attempt to listen lovingly to the Lord as well as to each other – to work out any differences which the enemy has caused during the heart-breaking years of serious dissension and alienation. Satan is shown in Scripture to be "a deceiver", a "robber" and "a thief"! He had tried to divide and disrupt the beautiful unity which had once existed in our VMTC International Family! Thousands of people had prayed over the three years for reconciliation – seemingly to no avail – but at last the Lord broke the enemy's power and *real* Victory in Jesus' Love is now on its way! Praise God from whom all blessings flow! We rejoice in the life changing Power of the Holy Spirit! "Thanks be to God, who gives us the victory through our Lord Jesus Christ." *(I Corinthians 15:57)*

This book would be incomplete if I did not review some of the Scriptural principles that the Lord was teaching me through these experiences – as VMTC Prayer Ministry grew in fulfillment of His many prophecies that were given to me on different occasions.

1) <u>The principle of forgiving others</u> – even when I was being verbally abused, betrayed or falsely accused or condemned – especially when I did not feel like doing so.

2) <u>The principle of repentance</u> – asking God to forgive us when we sinned against others, or ourselves, or against Him in thought, word or deed – even when we didn't feel like it!

3) <u>The principle of thanking God for the answer *before*</u> <u>the prayer request was fulfilled</u>, thanking Him in advance – even when the situation appeared to us to be hopeless.

4) <u>The principle of faith</u> – trusting *in* Him, believing *in* Him, having "the faith *of* the Son of God" – even

ADDENDUM TO CHAPTER XI

SATAN IS A ROBBER AND A THIEF

❦

Sadly, our hopes for reconciliation were dashed at our U. S. April Board of Directors' Meeting after a further unhappy exchange of letters with varying conditions! All of us were disheartened as we could not see any significant changes that would be necessary for real reconciliation. Subsequently, our Board decided that there was no longer any use for me to go with our two Delegates to the proposed September Meeting in Canada! Three months later, *the Holy Spirit began to work quietly* through the Australian Member of The Executive when he wrote me a beautiful note on a most meaningful card — and followed this up with a phone call from Canada on Thursday night — after I had replied suggesting that he come to the States to talk personally with our President Emeritus and me. As we tried to work out a suitable date (and found that nothing was available) we began to discuss serious past issues in a loving way — and ended with prayers that the Lord would "show us how" if He wanted Rev. Al Brock and me to make last minute plans to attend the Meeting in Canada on Monday! To our amazement, the two available airline schedules were perfect and the airfares were more reasonable than we had expected at such a late date! I called Al Brock and he said that his calendar was amazingly clear. He, also, felt that we should make one last effort to restore unity by changing our plans and flying to Hamilton, Ontario. In a call to our VMTC-USA President, we received his blessing for these altered plans. Miraculously, details began to fall into place and phone calls went through with amazing ease — *the impossible was happening and we were feeling at peace about the sudden, radical change in plans*! Despite loss of luggage, we made our very close connections and arrived at the lovely Holy Spirit Retreat Center in time for the beginning of the most important Meeting of The Executive which preceded the full Board Meeting.

At first, although we were lovingly welcomed by the four Members of The Executive, many tensions and "cross currents" still existed amongst us — *but we were all praying for the Holy Spirit to be the Enabler* who could bring us into loving unity in spite of some very real problems. Because of our differences in cultural backgrounds, there were differences in styles of leadership that had to be overcome. However, we were very aware of the undergirding of prayer coming from the eight countries represented at this International Board Meeting by their seventeen Delegates. Gradually, as decisions were made and Motions passed, we experienced the move of the Holy Spirit, giving us great wisdom, forgiveness and love for each other — expressed in a new and wonderful way! Suddenly, there was a time of melting and renewal as we were inspired to ask and receive forgiveness of each other under the guidance of the Holy Spirit. From then on, we were even more aware of the Lord's Purposes in bringing us all together in this last minute reconciliation! Problems began to be resolved as necessary changes were defined and accepted on all sides. Our worship services were truly meaningful at the beginning and ending of long days. Our fellowship at mealtimes was most enjoyable and important as questions could be asked and answered in a more open and constructive way. Some practical solutions miraculously took the place of former stumbling-blocks! Important suggestions for necessary changes were accepted lovingly as Motions were framed wisely and enthusiastically passed — so that we were all aware that we could work together in a new unity now — and in the future. VMTC-USA's Vice President was elected to be the Second Vice President of the International Board and he will join me (as Founder and Resource Person) in attending future Meetings of The Executive! Praise God! We ended those four days with an outpouring of the Holy Spirit in a beautiful Blessing Service in the Chapel as each Delegate prayed for the next one — and later, all of them prayed for the six of us on The Executive and for the President of the newly accepted country, VMTC-New Zealand. The Holy Spirit led me to pray the closing prayer of joyous thanksgiving for the wonderful miracle of the Lord's reconciliation that had transpired in our midst. Our final song was "Bind Us Together, Lord, With Cords That Shall Never Be Broken"! *Miracle of Miracles!!! Satan has been defeated!! Reconciliation had at last taken place in our VMTC Family!*

though problems seemed insurmountable.

5) <u>The principle of persevering in claiming Jesus'
Victory</u> – even when the answer was delayed and
Satan seemed to be thwarting God's Purposes.

6) <u>The principle of praying in Jesus' Name (literally in
His Nature) for *His* Will to be done</u> – acknowledging
His Name as higher than the name of "cancer" or
"Salmonella" or "heart failure" – even when the
doctor said it was incurable.

7) <u>The principle of claiming the Power of His shed
Blood, the Victory of Calvary, over the enemy's
attacks</u> – even when it looked as if Satan was winning
the battle.

8) <u>The principle of waiting on the Lord</u> – even when the
<u>answer tarried</u> – remembering that His ways are not
always our ways, and that His timing is perfect.

9) <u>The principle of expecting His miracles of provision
and protection</u> – even when the enemy, our adversary,
tried to discourage us from moving forward in Jesus'
Power.

10) <u>The principle of seeking intercessors to stand with us
against Satan's attempts to sift or discourage us</u> –
even when spirits of helplessness and hopelessness
threatened to engulf us.

11) <u>The principle of surrendering our wills, our loved
ones, our homes, our expectations, our work, our</u>

churches, and our "security blankets" – giving over total control to Jesus – even when we wanted to do our *own* thing in our *own* way!

12) The principle of focusing on the Lord's Purposes – being single minded, not swayed by self-will or the will of others – seeking what Jesus would think or say or do. *(Luke 11:34)*

13) The principle of yielding *total control* to Jesus when, like Paul , we ask Him to be "All in all."   He also wrote "For to me, to live is Christ, and to die is gain." *(Philippians 1:21)*

Will you join me in this prayer of Total Commitment to the Lord?

I SUBMIT MYSELF TODAY:

To God: My Heavenly Father, Creator and Deliverer;

To Jesus: My Savior, Healer and Redeemer;

To the Holy Spirit: My Guide, Sanctifier and Empowerer;

To the Word of God: As my rule of life.

I COMMIT MYSELF–MY SPIRIT, WILL, MIND,

EMOTIONS AND BODY TO JESUS MY LORD–

NOW AND FOREVER–THAT I MAY FULFILL HIS

PURPOSES FOR MY LIFE–THIS DAY AND FOREVER.

I DO THIS IN JOYFUL THANKSGIVING FOR ALL HE

HAS DONE FOR ME, IN ME AND THROUGH ME –

FOR HIS GLORY! Amen.

Notes

Notes

Notes

TRIAL BY FIRE: By Anne S. White

Another practical handbook offering valuable guidelines for the difficult aspects of our spiritual walk.

If you have passed from the "honeymoon stage" of your walk and have begun to experience the purging and pruning of the Lord, and have become aware of the reality of spiritual warfare...... this book is a must!

Missioner, Teacher, Counselor, Author of- *Jesus, All in All, Healing Adventure, Dayspring, The Transforming Power of God, Healing Devotions, Freed To Live, The Master Speaks Today,* & *Study Adventure in Trial By Fire.*

Anne S. White has given 30 years of her life to a lay ministry of writing, counseling, teaching, speaking, and sharing Christ in Churches of other denominations as well as in her own Episcopal Church. Her extensive preparation and experience in the work of VMTC Prayer Ministry and ministry to the sick at heart have fitted her to speak with authority, particularly on "Divine Healing", "Spiritual Warfare", "Total Commitment", "The Lordship of Jesus Christ", and "The Baptism in the Holy Spirit".

As an ecumenical Episcopalian, Mrs. White rejoices at the opportunity to work with all fellow Christians to fulfill the Lord's commission: "Go preach the Kingdom, heal the sick". Her emphasis is on the need for healing of key relationships, of sick minds, emotions, spirits and bodies; so that men may become whole in deeper commitment to Jesus Christ -- their Lord, Savior, Redeemer, Healer, and Baptizer. Her lay ministry has been protected, empowered and extended by the Lord through years of spiritual warfare -which have equipped her to write *Trial by Fire!*

$3.95 plus postage   **ISBN 0-89228-0445-X**

Order from:

IMPACT CHRISTIAN BOOKS
332 Leffingwell Ave. Suite 101. Kirkwood, MO 63122

or:
VICTORIOUS MINISTRY THROUGH CHRIST
P.O. Box 1804. Winter Park, FL 32792, 407/657-4893

STUDY ADVENTURE FOR TRIAL BY FIRE

More Meat for Men--by Anne S. White and Don Vanzant

Using this STUDY ADVENTURE will make Anne's practical book, TRIAL BY FIRE, come alive in an even more effective way! After your "mountaintop experiences", learn *how* to "hold your victory" in spiritual warfare and how to *grow* in total commitment -- in order to overcome Satan's attacks. As the Lord uses them to develop character in you, He brings good out of what the enemy intended for evil.

"Far too many Christians fail to walk in victory. They either 'perish for a lack of knowledge' or they 'fail to walk in the Light as He is in the Light'. Either the lack of information concerning the depth of the Christian faith or the failure to be persevering in the practice of Christian discipline is sufficient to destroy the average Christian. This STUDY ADVENTURE for Anne White's book, TRIAL BY FIRE provides an adequate learning tool to impart the knowledge concerning the victorious life that wins over satanic forces that attempt to destroy us. It also provides the motivation that can lead us to disciplined victorious living. This teaching tool is an appropriate resource for instruction in spiritual warfare and Christ-like living. I heartily recommend the use of the 'STUDY ADVENTURE' ". -- Rev. Vernon Stoop.

"I have used the STUDY ADVENTURE for TRIAL BY FIRE by Anne S. White and Don Vanzant as a homework assignment for adult Confirmation Class. What a perfect vehicle to point to tools for victorious living through the 'Lordship of Jesus', the 'Baptism in the Holy Spirit', 'Spiritual Warfare', 'Repentance', and 'How to Pray with Power'! This workbook helps new and mature Christians in their discipleship with obtainable goals of understanding over a period of a few weeks. Coupled with Bible study and good doctrine courses, your members should gain the proper balance needed for victorious living in the world today". -- The Rev. Clifford Horvath.

$1.95 plus postage   **ISBN 0-89228-102-2**

Order from:

IMPACT CHRISTIAN BOOKS
332 Leffingwell Ave. Suite 101, Kirkwood, MO 63122

or:
VICTORIOUS MINISTRY THROUGH CHRIST
P.O. Box 1804, Winter Park, FL 32792. 407/657-4893

JESUS, ALL IN ALL

"It flows....It challenges....It communicates the Gospel.... It's Anne White's best book so far." -- **The Rev. Alva H. Brock, VMTC President Emeritus**

Anne S. White has given over 30 years of her life to a lay ministry of writing, counseling, teaching, speaking, and sharing Christ in churches of many denominations, Her extensive preparation and experience in the work of VMTC Prayer Ministry and other ministries have fitted her to write with real authority. As an ecumenical Episcopalian, Mrs. White rejoices at every opportunity to serve with all fellow Christians who are carrying out our Lord's Commission to His early disciples: "observe all that I have commanded you....". Her emphasis is on the need for healing of relationships, of sick minds, emotions, spirits and bodies so that men may become whole in deeper commitment to Jesus Christ -- their Lord, Savior, Redeemer, Healer, and Baptizer. Many have found healing as they read her books.

Since June 1972, the Lord has guided and provided for her to take clergy and lay teams with her to minister in England, Sweden, Finland, Norway, Australia, Canada, Manila, Malaysia, Singapore, and Pakistan -- to set up Clergy Schools of Prayer Ministry and/or Missions and Retreats. She has spoken (along with other outstanding leaders) at many large, annual Church Renewal Conferences in England and Australia as well as in the USA -- including regional Episcopal Charismatic Fellowship Conferences and Women's Aglow International Conferences. In the course of this extended ministry, Anne has circled the globe ten times. All income from her lay ministry has subsidized Prayer Ministry Schools in the USA and abroad.

$4.95 plus postage   **ISBN 0-9605178-0-4**

Order from:

IMPACT BOOKS
332 Leffingwell Ave. Suite 101, Kirkwood, MO 63122

or:
VICTORIOUS MINISTRY THROUGH CHRIST
P.O. Box 1804, Winter Park, FL 32790, 407/657-4893

DAYSPRING
A Book of Prophecies and Scriptures

Meaningful for Today!
Originally published by LOGOS

The Master speaks to His disciples through the Word of God and through the inspiration of His Holy Spirit. He illumines our minds and encourages us through prophecies, through the word of Wisdom and the word of Knowledge. Some of these writings were given by Him to this listener early one morning as I entered into a particularly difficult chapter of life. They have been tested and found helpful in the laboratory of life. They are shared with the prayer that others too may find strength for the day as they pause each morning to meditate on the selected Scriptures and to listen for the Voice of the Master through these prophecies. He teaches, He comforts, He strengthens, He guides, He exhorts His disciples today -- "forthtelling His good News"!

"Anne White is one of the few who have learned to listen as well as to speak to God, and this has proved of great importance in her gifted healing ministry. She has also learned how to listen to people. Prophecy should always be judged by Scripture. But God *does* speak today through prophecies -- as He did in the days of the apostles -- always confirming, never contradicting the Scriptures. I hope that many will use these readings and prophecies -- one for each day of the year -- in addition to their regular devotional habits; and that they will not limit the Holy Spirit, but expect Him to speak to them in ways, in addition to these written prophecies. Above all else, I trust this book will teach us all to be better *listeners*. I believe it will." ...

The Rev. Canon Michael Harper, London, England.

$4.95 plus postage   **ISBN 0-9605178-2- 0**

Order from:

IMPACT CHRISTIAN BOOKS
332 Leffingwell Ave. Suite 101, Kirkwood, MO 63122

or:

VICTORIOUS MINISTRY THROUGH CHRIST
P.O. Box 1804, Winter Park, FL 32792, 407/657-4893

FREED TO LIVE

Anne S. White has committed her life to being refined --and enabling others to be refined -- so that the Love of Jesus may be more gloriously seen! She has compiled a vast knowledge of means of handling the trials and tribulations that often come to us all in life. Her concise, clear and accurate presentation enables us as Christians to grow in our life of liberty in Jesus.

This book not only helps to identify some root causes but also marks the way through the fiery furnace, so that we can become a part of God's mighty army at work in the world today to set captives free. -- Rev. William W. Westlund, Pastor, First Presbyterian Church, Belvidere, IL, is also President VMTC-USA.

+++

"Anne S. White's Ministry is a vital one for clergy and missionaries --and also for people at all levels in the Church of Pakistan. This Ministry brings dramatic changes in our work with drug addicts as we have seen a significant breakthrough in this area. Since Mrs. White first visited us in 1981, the work of Renewal and the Healing Ministry of the Church have increased remarkably in Pakistan". -- The Rt. Rev. Arne Rudvin, Bishop, Diocese of Karachi, Church of Pakistan.

+++

$4.95 plus postage   **ISBN 0-9605178-3-9**

Order from:

IMPACT CHRISTIAN BOOKS, INC.
322 Leffingwell Ave., Suite 101, Kirkwood, MO 63122

or:

VICTORIOUS MINISTRY THROUGH CHRIST, INC.
P.O. Box 1804, Winter Park, FL 32790 (407/657-4893)

HEALING ADVENTURE

About the Author:

Mrs. Anne S. White is the Founder and Executive Vice-President of Victorious Ministry Through Christ, Inc. She has been used throughout the USA and in many countries abroad as a conference speaker as well as a seminar and retreat leader for both clergy and laity. Her lay ministry is licensed under the authority of her Rector and the Bishop of the Episcopal Diocese of Central Florida -- as well as Victorious Ministry Through Christ, an ecumenical Board of Directors, composed of eleven ordained ministers who are deeply committed to using this very effective, Scriptural, balanced and accountable work of the Holy Spirit to bring healing and wholeness to people in their churches. The emphasis is on total commitment to Jesus Christ. God uses VMTC ministry to help people win Victory in today's spiritual warfare!

A Three Day Clergy School of VMTC Prayer Ministry:

These Schools are for ordained ministers and their spouses baptized in the Holy Spirit (or desiring to be) who feel called by God to be used in this ministry of healing the whole person. A local pastor assists the staff , 10 trained VMTC Prayer Ministers, including two members of the Board of Directors. Lay people may come after the pastor has attended one School. HEALING ADVENTURE is required reading for all those desiring to attend a VMTC Training School.

$4.95   ISBN 0-960-5178-5-0

Order from:

IMPACT CHRISTIAN BOOKS, INC.
322 LEFFINGWELL, SUITE 101, KIRKWOOD, MO 63122

or:

VICTORIOUS MINISTRY THROUGH CHRIST, INC.
P.O. BOX 1804, WINTER PARK, FL 32790 (407/657-4893)

HEALING DEVOTIONS

A Revised Edition, By Anne S. White

Published by Morehouse Barlow
A Sequel to HEALING ADVENTURE

This book may appeal to you because it is different from most devotional books. It is charismatic in every sense and will stimulate your understanding in respect to your own deepest needs and problems. It will help you to grow in faith as the Scriptures used become alive to you! And the simple prayers in "non-Churchy" language will encourage you to pray more spontaneously with new reality.

"The reading of HEALING DEVOTIONS has set my spirit singing and has given me new insights into God's power and will to heal today. I predict that, like Anne White's other books, God will use this one to bring restoration of the healing ministry to today's Church. To read it daily (with Scripture and hymnbook in hand) will, I believe, lead you toward greater 'wholeness' in Christ... May the Holy Spirit use it to bring you deeper healing and guide you in your commitment to Jesus. May the gifts of the Spirit be lavished upon you, the fruit of the Spirit grow in you, and may you go on from victory to victory with a 'singing faith' ". -- The Rev. Alva H. Brock, VMTC Director.

$4.95 plus postage   **ISBN 0-9605178-4-7**

Order from:

IMPACT CHRISTIAN BOOKS, INC.
332 Leffingwell Ave. Suite 101, Kirkwood, MO 63122

or:
VICTORIOUS MINISTRY THROUGH CHRIST, INC.
P.O. Box 1804, Winter Park, FL 32792, 407/657-4893

THE MASTER SPEAKS TODAY

Scriptures and Prophecies for Daily Listening to the Lord

"I have been privileged to work with Anne S. White in the VMTC Prayer Ministry since 1970. I enthusiastically recommend this anointed book. It is fitting that she should offer a second book of prophecies --for Anne is a deeply committed, disciplined, wise Christian woman who has faithfully prayed for and listened to the Lord's guidance. Many of the prophecies given to Anne so many years ago in DAYSPRING have been fulfilled! I believe this second book will be especially helpful as the Holy Spirit guides the readers to find the right message on the day it is needed.". . . Rev. Alva H. Brock, a Director of Victorious Ministry Through Christ.
++++++++++++++++++++++

"Listening to the Lord for the purpose of sharing prophecies is something like being encouraged by no less a person than St. Paul when he said: 'Follow the way of love and eagerly desire spiritual gifts, especially the gift of prophecy. ... Everyone who prophesies speaks to men for their strengthening, encouragement and comfort'. (I Corinthians 14:1, 3). The Scripturally based prophecies contained in this devotional writing, reinforce Paul's exhortation. They bring a welcome refreshment of stable, corrective prophetic words (reinforced by Scripture) in a time lacking in moral absolutes ." . . . . Rev. Vernon Stoop, Jr., Sr. Pastor, Shepherd of the Hills United Church of Christ, Sassamansville, PA, and Sec'y/Treasurer, North American Renewal Services Committee, is a former Member of VTMC's Board of Directors.
++++++++++++++++++++++

"Anne S. White's Ministry continues to be a gift of the Holy Spirit to His Church. In her book, THE MASTER SPEAKS TODAY, the Holy Spirit prophetically speaks to the issues of our hearts and our faithful commitment to Christ. The Spirit will lead you to victory as you read this book in your daily life." . . . Rev. John P. Nyhan, Rector of St. James the Just Church, Franklin Square, NY, is also a valued Member of VMTC's Board of Directors.

$4.95   **ISBN 0-9605178-5-5**

Order from:
IMPACT CHRISTIAN BOOKS, INC.
332 Leffingwell, Suite 101, Kirkwood, MO 63122
or:
VICTORIOUS MINISTRY THROUGH CHRIST, INC.
P.O. Box 1804, Winter Park, FL 32790 (407/657-4893)

TO ORDER BOOKS
by ANNE S. WHITE

send your order with a check or money
order including postage to:

VICTORIOUS MINISTRY
THROUGH CHRIST, INC.
POST OFFICE BOX 1804
WINTER PARK, FLORIDA 32790
407-657-4893

HEALING ADVENTURE ---------------------- *$4.95*

TRIAL BY FIR E ------------------------------- *$3.50*

Study Adventure in TRIAL BY FIRE -------- *$1.95*

DAYSPRING ------------------------------------- *$4.95*

TRANSFORMING POWER OF GOD ------- *$1.50*

JESUS, ALL IN ALL -------------------------- *$3.95*

FREED TO LIVE ------------------------------- *$4.95*

HEALING DEVOTIONS ---------------------- *$4.95*

THE MASTER SPEAKS TODAY ------------- *$4.95*

Special on Prepaid Orders:
Ten or more books: 25 % discount!!
(Be sure to add postage & Handling)
Make checks payable to Victorious Ministry Through Christ
Shipping: 1-2 Books $2.50; 3-5 Books $3.50; 6-9 Books $4.50
10-15 Books $5.50

FOR ADDITIONAL COPIES WRITE:

Impac Chris ian Books

332 Leffingwell Ave., Suite 101
Kirkwood, MO 63122

AVAILABLE AT YOUR LOCAL BOOKSTORE, OR YOU MAY ORDER DIRECTLY. Toll-Free, order-line only M/C, DISC, or VISA 1-800-451-2708.